A Brief Introduction to the Semitic Languages

Gorgias Handbooks

19

Series Editor
George Anton Kiraz

The Gorgias Handbooks series provides students and scholars with textbooks and reference books useful for the classroom and for research.

A Brief Introduction to the Semitic Languages

Aaron D. Rubin

gorgias press
2010

Gorgias Press LLC, 954 River Road, Piscataway, NJ, 08854, USA

www.gorgiaspress.com

2010

ISBN 978-1-61719-860-1 **ISSN 1935-6838**

Library of Congress Cataloging-in-Publication Data

Rubin, Aaron D., 1976-

A brief introduction to the Semitic languages / by Aaron D. Rubin.

p. cm. -- (Gorgias handbooks; 19)

Includes bibliographical references.

1. Semitic languages--Grammar, Comparative. I. Title.

PJ3021.R823 2010

492'.045--dc22

2010027121

Printed and bound by CPI Group (UK) Ltd, Croydon, CR0 4YY

TABLE OF CONTENTS

PREFACE

The contents of this book were originally intended to form a single chapter in a larger work on the Afroasiatic languages. When that project fell through, I decided that what I had written was worth publishing on its own. I had already been using it in seminars as an introduction to the Semitic family, and students found it useful. I expanded the original work, and this book is the result.

A comparative study of the Semitic languages is a very substantial undertaking, as the family comprises dozens of languages, spread out among the ancient, medieval, and modern periods. Numerous comprehensive studies have been made (see Chapter 6, below), and much more still needs to be written. But these larger works are much more than introductions to the Semitic family. There are also numerous brief sketches of the Semitic family, ranging from a few pages to a few dozen pages. These are more appropriate for the beginner or non-specialist, but they lack adequate detail to be very useful. This survey, therefore, is something of a middle ground between these two types. Its aim is to be both practical and manageable.

This brief introduction is intended to provide the student, general linguist, or amateur language enthusiast with an overview of the characteristic features of the Semitic languages, as well as some of the more interesting and unique developments that take place in the individual languages. Moreover, it is my goal to give the reader an idea of the diversity of the Semitic languages, as well as their similarities. All too often, sketches of this family focus mainly on the classical languages, and so in this book I have tried to incorporate at least as many examples from modern languages (particularly lesser known languages) as there are from ancient languages. I want the reader to know that the Semitic family includes numerous vibrant and fascinating modern languages, worthy of all sorts of linguistic studies.

In order to make all of the examples as clear as possible, I have provided morpheme-by-morpheme glossing, following the Leipzig Glossing Rules. I assume that the reader is familiar with linguistic terminology, and has a basic understanding of historical linguistics. For those who do not have this background, I have provided some references to general linguistic works in the Guide to Further Reading (Chapter 6).

Given the length of this volume, many topics have necessarily been left unexplored (or underexplored), but I hope that the Guide to Further Reading (Chapter 6), as well as the many references scattered throughout the book, will encourage the reader to pursue the study of the Semitic languages further. With such a long attested history, such a diversity of languages—including languages that are important to several major religions and to some of history's most influential cultures—the study of the Semitic languages is exceptionally rewarding. And while I do not expect that everyone should choose a career devoted to the study of the Semitic languages, I do hope that everyone can appreciate their importance to both the past and present.

ACKNOWLEDGEMENTS

My sincere thanks are due to my teacher and friend John Huehnergard, whose influence is obvious throughout this volume.

My thanks also to Gary Rendsburg and Rebecca Hasselbach, who provided me with very valuable comments on earlier drafts of this book. I am also grateful to Dr. George Kiraz, who accepted this book into the Gorgias Handbooks series.

My wife Kim has, once again, dedicated a large amount of time to editing this book in its various stages, and her assistance has been invaluable. I thank her, as always, with love and great appreciation.

Abbreviations

1	first person
2	second person
3	third person
ACC	accusative
ACT	active
ADJ	adjective
BCE	before the common era
C	common gender
C	consonant
ca.	*circa*
CE	common era
COLL	collective
COMPAR	comparative
CONJ	conjunction
CONSTR	construct
DAT	dative
Deut.	Deuteronomy
DN	Divine Name
DU	dual
Exod.	Exodus
EXIST	existential particle
F	feminine
FUT	future
Gen.	Genesis
GEN	genitive
GER	gerund
IMPER	imperative
INDEF	indefinite
INF	infinitive
INTERROG	interrogative
JUSS	jussive

lit.	literally
M	masculine
NEG	negative
NENA	Northeastern Neo-Aramaic
NOM	nominative
NONPAST	non-past (present or future)
Num.	Numbers
OBJ	object
PART	participle
PASS	passive
PAST	past tense
PL	plural
PREP	preposition
PRES	present
PROG	progressive
REL	relative pronoun
SG	singular
SUBORD	subordinating particle
V	verb; vowel
X > Y	X develops into Y.
X < Y	X derives from Y.
*	An asterisk marks a reconstructed or underlying form. For languages whose vocalization is not indicated in the script (e.g., Ugaritic), an asterisk also marks a theoretical vocalized form.
**	A double asterisk indicates a non-existent or ungrammatical form.

INTRODUCTION

With a written history of nearly five thousand years, the Semitic languages comprise one of the world's earliest attested and longest attested language families. Most of the Semitic languages were or are spoken in the areas of the Levant, Mesopotamia, Arabia, and across the Red Sea in Ethiopia and Eritrea. Small pockets of Phoenician speakers settled in North Africa in the first millennium BCE (where their language is referred to as Punic), but it was not until the spread of Islam, and its language Arabic, that much of North Africa became Semitic speaking.

Today, Arabic is the most important of the Semitic languages, as it is the *lingua franca* of the Near East and North Africa. With roughly two hundred million speakers, it is also (by far) the Semitic language with the greatest number of speakers. Two thousand years ago, Aramaic was the *lingua franca* of the Near East, and a thousand years earlier, Akkadian had this distinction. The Semitic languages are thus inextricably linked to this region that is often called the cradle of civilization, and that still today is the subject of much international attention.

Two of the Semitic languages, Hebrew and Arabic, are the holy languages of major religions, Judaism and Islam, respectively. A third language, Aramaic, has played a significant role in the histories of both Christianity and Judaism. As such, these languages have been widely studied for many centuries. In fact, the relationship of Arabic, Hebrew, and Aramaic was recognized already in the 9th century by the Jewish grammarian Judah ibn Quraysh. Comparative Semitic studies has a long history indeed.

With the coming of the Reformation in Europe, and the consequent focus on the original languages of the Bible, the study of Hebrew became very popular among Christians. In the following centuries, with the rise in popularity of the study of Arabic, and with the European discovery of other Semitic languages like Syriac and Ge'ez, came a rise in linguistic comparison of these languages. When the modern field of historical linguistics was developed in the 19th century for Indo-European studies, it was natural then that the methods were quickly applied to the Semitic languages.

The Semitic languages, both ancient and modern, continue to be widely studied. They play a role in many areas of academic study, such as linguistics, religious studies, history, political science, comparative literature, and others. Some of the languages have died out, and others are spoken by tiny, vanishing communities, yet many continue to grow and thrive as languages of both literature and daily communication. One must keep in mind that the Semitic family is continually evolving, and that no study can ever be the last word.

1 LANGUAGES AND CLASSIFICATION

The Semitic language family is part of a larger family of languages called Afroasiatic, which in older literature is also called Hamito-Semitic. Afroasiatic can be divided into the following branches:

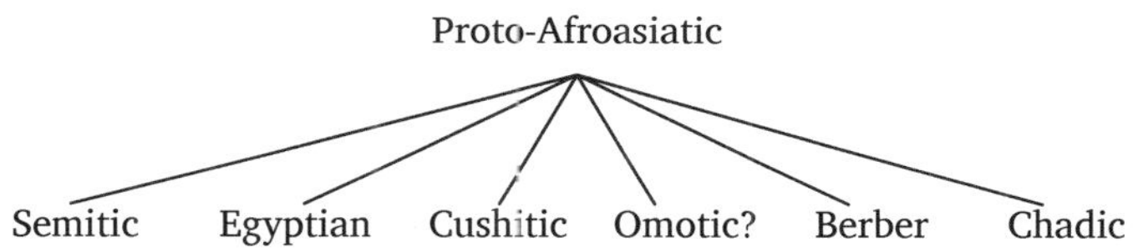

The existence of this macro-family has been recognized and studied since the 19th century, but given the great time depth that separates these branches, comparative Afroasiatic studies are tremendously difficult. Even the branches attested in antiquity, Semitic and Egyptian (both attested in the third millennium BCE), are highly divergent, suggesting a long period of separation. It does seem that some of the branches of Afroasiatic (e.g., Semitic and Egyptian, Semitic and Berber) share a greater number of similarities than do some other branches, but as yet it is impossible to demonstrate distinct sub-branches within the Afroasiatic family tree. Note that with the exception of Semitic, all of the branches of Afroasiatic are native to Africa: Egyptian, Cushitic, and Omotic in the east, and Chadic and Berber in the west. Also note that the position of the Omotic languages is still debated; some may really belong to the Cushitic family, and some of the languages may not even be Afroasiatic at all.

Within the Semitic family of languages, there is no consensus among scholars with regards to the proper subgrouping of the Semitic family, and probably there never will be. The following presentation reflects the subgrouping of the Semitic family as it is best understood given the facts available to date. For a detailed discussion of the internal classification of Semitic, see Rubin (2008) and the many sources cited therein.

There is a primary division between East and West Semitic, a division that has remained relatively uncontroversial for more than a century.

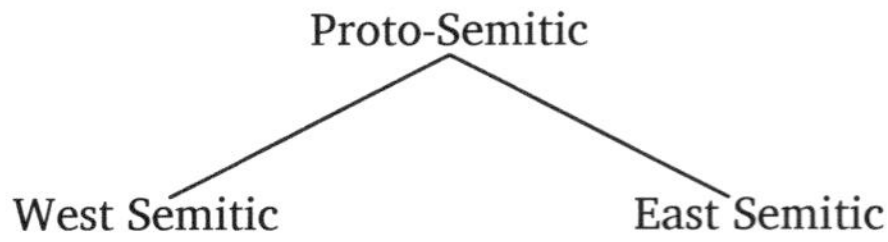

The foundation for this division is a major innovation that took place in the verbal system of West Semitic. In West Semitic, the inherited prefixed past tense (*yaqtul*) was replaced by the suffixed-conjugation (*qatala*), which in East Semitic functions as a stative (or verbal adjective). This shared development of a stative into a past tense, and the replacement (or marginalization) of the inherited past tense, is a defining characteristic of West Semitic, though there are, of course, other innovations that are specific to each of these two branches; see Huehnergard (2006b) for further discussion of East Semitic innovations.

Among the West Semitic languages, there is a division between the Central Semitic languages, the Ethiopian Semitic languages, and the Modern South Arabian languages.

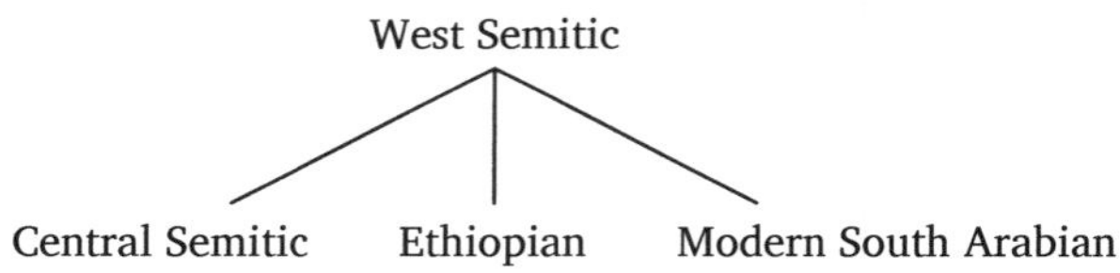

Central Semitic was first defined as such by Hetzron (1974, 1976), based largely on the development of a new imperfective verbal form (*yaqtulu*). This new form completely replaced the inherited imperfective form of the pattern *yVqattVl*, which survived in East Semitic, Ethiopian Semitic, and Modern South Arabian. The most detailed treatment of Central Semitic to date is that of Huehnergard (2005a). The Central Semitic family comprises Arabic, including Classical Arabic and other ancient North Arabian dialects, as well as a multitude of (often mutually unintelligible) modern Arabic dialects; the four Ṣayhadic languages, also known as the Old South Arabian languages; and the Northwest Semitic languages.

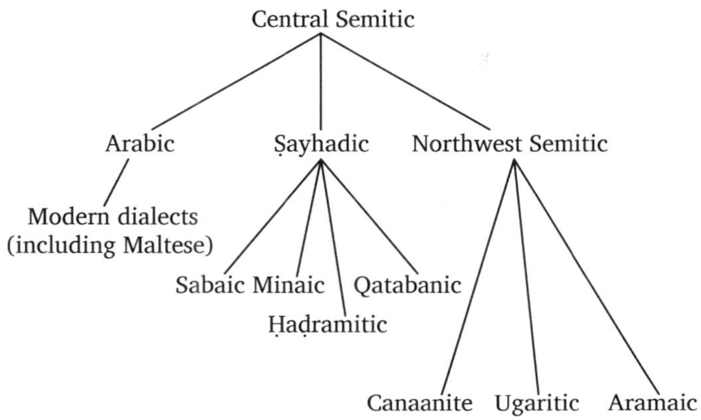

Note that in addition to Ugaritic, Canaanite, and Aramaic, there are two other dialects of Northwest Semitic, attested in inscriptions from the first millennium BCE. One is called Sam'alian, known from just a few monumental inscriptions from ancient Sam'al, which is the site of modern Zincirli in south-central Turkey (about 75 miles northeast of Antakya). These texts date from about 820–730 BCE. The other Northwest Semitic dialect, which is given no special name, is known from a single inscription found at the site of Deir 'Allā, in northwestern Jordan (about 30 miles northwest of Amman). This inscription, which contains only about thirty broken lines of text, dates from about the same time period as the Sam'alian texts. The exact position of Sam'alian dialect and the dialect of the Deir 'Allā inscription within Northwest Semitic is unclear, but based on the scanty evidence that we possess, it seems that they cannot be called Canaanite, Ugaritic, or Aramaic.

Details regarding dates of attestation and location, as well as further information on the subgrouping of some of the individual branches of Central Semitic, will be given in the following sections. Following is a more complete Semitic family tree, combining what has been presented so far. In this tree, the numbers in parentheses indicate the subsections below in which the language or language group is treated. Languages (or groups) that are no longer spoken are indicated by italics.

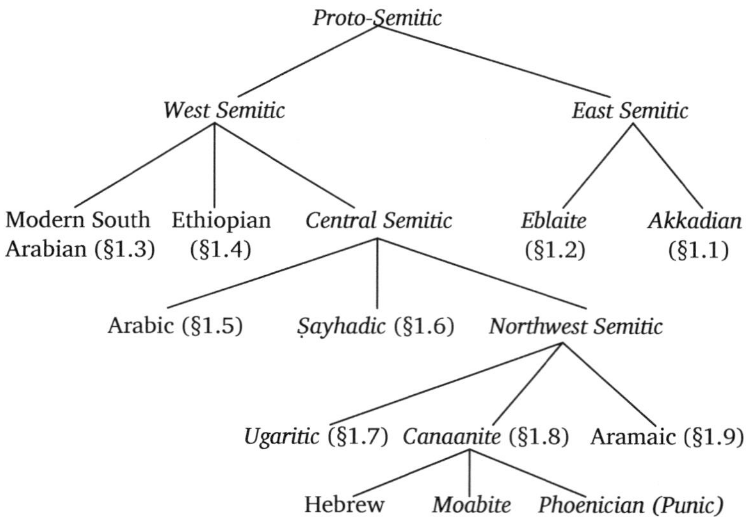

1.1 AKKADIAN

Akkadian was spoken by the ancient Babylonians and Assyrians in Mesopotamia, more or less in the area of modern Iraq. It is the oldest attested Semitic language, with written records already around 2400 BCE. Akkadian is not a uniform language, but rather can be divided into multiple dialects, many of which achieved a standardized written form. The major division is between the Babylonian and Assyrian dialects, which in turn are distinguished chronologically. Following are the major dialects, along with their approximate dates of attestation:

Old Akkadian	(2400–2000 BCE)
Old Babylonian / Old Assyrian	(2000–1500 BCE)
Middle Babylonian / Middle Assyrian	(1500–1000 BCE)
Neo-Babylonian / Neo-Assyrian	(1000–600 BCE)
Late Babylonian	(600 BCE–100 CE)

Already in the Middle Babylonian period, Old Babylonian came to be considered the classical period of Akkadian. Authors in both Assyria and Babylonia developed a purely literary dialect based on the Old Babylonian model, known as Standard Bayblonian. Standard Bayblonian was used for literary and some monumental texts in all later periods. Some time in the first half of the first millennium BCE, Akkadian died out as a spoken language, though Late and Standard Babylonian continued to be used in writing until about 100 CE.

There are also what are called "peripheral" dialects of Akkadian, which are essentially dialects attested outside of the Babylonian and Assyrian homelands, usually reflecting substrate influence from the local language. Notable sites where peripheral Akkadian texts have been found include Nuzi, Alalakh, Mari, Emar, Ugarit, and El-Amarna (see §1.8). These come mainly from the mid- to late second millennium BCE, when Akkadian was used as a *lingua franca* throughout the Near East.

Knowledge of the cuneiform system used to write Akkadian died out by the 2nd century CE, and cuneiform was deciphered only in the 19th century.

1.2 EBLAITE

Eblaite designates the language of ancient Ebla, modern Tell Mardikh, which lies just south of Aleppo, Syria. The language was discovered only in the 1970s, when several thousand cuneiform tablets were excavated at the site. All of the texts can be dated to a period that spans less than a century, from the late 24th to the mid-23rd century BCE. Because of the nature of the cuneiform writing system used for Eblaite—in particular the broad use of logograms and the ambiguity in the representation of nearly all consonants and vowels—knowledge of the language remains patchy. Still, it is clear that it is a close relative of Akkadian, but with enough differences to warrant placing it in its own branch of East Semitic (Huehnergard 2006b).

1.3 MODERN SOUTH ARABIAN

The Modern South Arabian family includes six languages: Mehri, Jibbali (or Śḥeri), Ḥarsusi, Soqoṭri, Hobyot, and Baṭḥari. All are spoken in eastern Yemen and western Oman, with the exception of Soqoṭri, which is spoken on the Yemeni-governed island of Soqoṭra, located in the Indian Ocean about 150 miles east of the Horn of Africa. Mehri, Jibbali, and Soqoṭri in turn have a number of dialects; in fact, Ḥarsusi and Baṭḥari are simliar enough to

Mehri that they may also be considered dialects of that language. Each of these languages has a relatively small number of speakers, though exact figures are unknown. Mehri is the language with the greatest number of speakers; estimates on this number range from about 75,000 to 150,000. Jibbali has perhaps 30,000 speakers, Soqoṭri has perhaps 10,000 speakers, and the remaining three languages have probably less than a thousand speakers each.

None of these languages has a tradition of writing, and so our knowledge of these languages is quite recent. A couple are documented by Europeans as early as the 1830s, while others are known only from the 20th century. Hobyot and Baṭḥari remain especially poorly documented.

Despite the confusing terminology, the Modern South Arabian languages did not descend from the languages sometimes known as Old South Arabian (see below, §1.6), nor are they varieties of Arabic.

Little has been done with the classification of the Modern South Arabian group. Lonnet (2006) provides a tentative classification scheme:

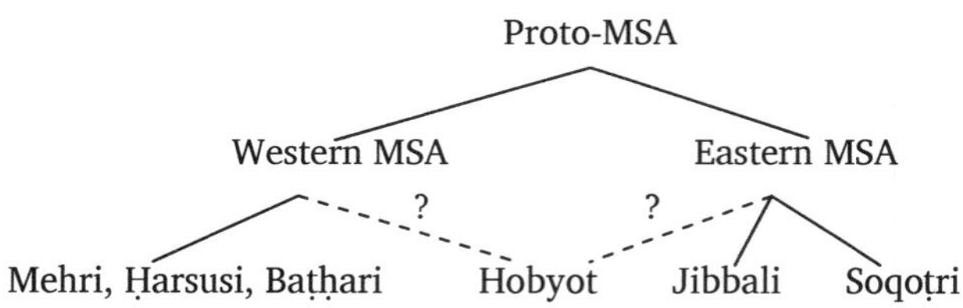

1.4 ETHIOPIAN SEMITIC

The Ethiopian branch of Semitic contains a variety of languages, most of which are known only from modern times. The major exception is Ge'ez, the classical language of Ethiopia and still the liturgical language of the Ethiopian Church, which is attested in inscriptions already in the early 4th century CE, or perhaps even in the late 3rd century CE. Amharic is attested from the 14th century CE, but was not widely written until the 19th century. Though some of the languages still await comprehensive description, the Ethiopian Semitic family has on the whole been well studied, as has its internal classification. Following is a simplified family tree of the languages, modelled after the work of Hetzron (1972). Those languages that are no longer spoken are indicated with italics:

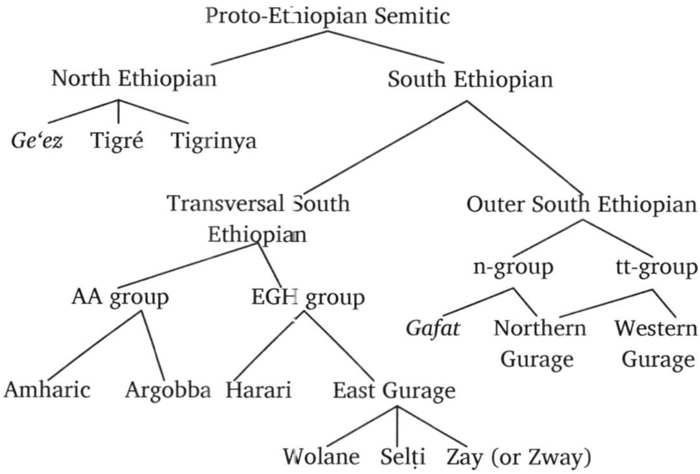

Ge'ez, the language of the ancient Kingdom of Axum, in Northern Ethiopia, probably died out as a spoken language close to a thousand years ago, but remained the primary written language of Ethiopia up to the 20th century. Tigrinya is spoken in the northern parts of Ethiopia, as well as in Eritrea, where it is the national language. It has about six million speakers total. Tigré is also spoken in Eritrea, where it has about a million speakers. Dahalik, spoken by the several thousand inhabitants of the Dahlak Archipelago, off the coast of Eritrea, may be a Tigré dialect, but some have claimed that it should be considered an independent language (Simeone-Senelle 2006).

Amharic is the most widely spoken Ethiopian Semitic language, and the second most widely spoken (after Arabic) of any Semitic language today. It is the national language and *lingua franca* of Ethiopia, where it has about 20 million native speakers, though it is understood by many more non-native speakers. The closely-related Argobba, spoken mainly in the Ankober region, about 100 miles northeast of Addis Ababa, has about 10,000 to 15,000 speakers remaining. Harari has perhaps 30,000 speakers. It was historically spoken only in the walled

Muslim city of Harar, in southeastern Ethiopia, but as a consequence of the political upheavals of the 1970s, most Harari speakers now live in the vicinity of Addis Ababa.

The remaining Ethiopian Semitic languages, other than Gafat, which became extinct in the mid-20th century, are often called together the "Gurage Languages", though, as illustrated in the above tree, they do not form a single genetic group. The Northern Gurage group contains three languages/dialects, while the Western Gurage group (which can be further subdivided) contains about ten. Speakers of the Gurage languages, totalling between one and two million, all live in the same region, about 150 miles southwest of Addis Ababa, and most of them are also grouped together ethnically. Thus for geographical and ethnic reasons, it is convenient to speak of the Gurage languages as a group. The Gurage languages form a Semitic island surrounded by speakers of Cushitic languages.

Those Ethiopian languages that are written all use a unique syllabary, based on the alphabet borrowed from the Sabeans. The exception is Harari, which has traditionally been written with the Arabic script; since the 1990s, however, the Ethiopian script has been used to write Harari.

1.5 ARABIC

Arabic today has roughly 200 million speakers, whose domain stretches from Mauritania in the west to Oman in the east. In Africa, it is the main language of all the North African countries, from Mauritania to Egypt, as well as in the northern regions of Chad and Sudan, and is also widely spoken in Djibouti and Eritrea. It is the main language of all the countries of the Middle East, with the exception of Turkey, Iran, and Israel. Still, it is widely spoken in Israel and is spoken in small pockets of Turkey and Iran. There are also Arabic-speaking communities in Central Asia (Afghanistan and Uzbekistan). In the Mediterranean, we find Maltese (see below) and a tiny community of speakers on Cyprus. In the Middle Ages, there were thriving Arabic-speaking communities in Iberia and in Sicily. Arabic is also spoken today by large expatriate communities in Europe and the Americas, and is the liturgical language of hundreds of millions of Muslims around the world.

Arabic is not a single linguistic entity, and we can distinguish different types of Arabic both chronologically and geographically. First, we must distinguish Arabic from what is known as Ancient North Arabian.

Proto-Arabic
Arabic   Ancient North Arabian

Ancient North Arabian is a cover term for several closely related dialects that are attested in inscriptions found mainly in the territories that are now Syria, Jordan, and Saudi Arabia, and that date from about the 8th century BCE to the 4th century CE. The names of these dialects include Taymanitic, Dadanitic, Dumaitic, Safaitic, Hismaic, Hasaitic, and Thamudic. Ancient North Arabian is attested about a millennium before Arabic, but none of these dialects are the ancestor of Arabic. Ancient North Arabian should be considered distinct from, though closely related to, the language that would become Classical Arabic.

For Arabic proper, we can distinguish several periods. Old Arabic designates the language of Arabic inscriptions, from about the 3rd to 7th centuries CE, that is, until the Islamic period. Old Arabic is relatively sparsely attested, and is found written in a variety of scripts. Classical Arabic refers to the variety of the written language that was standardized by the 8th century CE, based on the Qur'an and other pre-Islamic poetry. This has essentially remained the literary standard since, at least in terms of its grammar. Modern Standard Arabic (in Arabic, *fuṣḥā*) is essentially a modernized version of Classical Arabic that began to take shape in the 19th century. Not surprisingly, Modern Standard Arabic differs most from Classical Arabic in its lexicon, though there are also some minor differences in grammar. Modern Standard Arabic is the official language of the twenty-two Arab nations. It is the language of education, mass media, formal writing, and is used as a *lingua franca* across the Arab world.

While Modern Standard Arabic is the main written language of the Arab world, there exists a large number of spoken Arabic dialects, on which more will be said below. Many of the differences that exist among the modern dialects certainly existed already a millennium ago, though in literary (Classical Arabic) works, this fact is largely concealed. However, there are a very large number of texts from the medieval and early modern periods in which post-classical, non-standard features abound. These kinds of texts are loosely called Middle Arabic, and essentially form a sort of middle ground between the literary language and the spoken dialects.

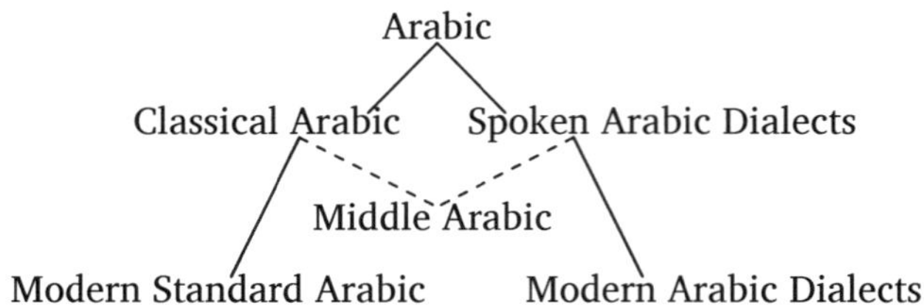

The spoken varieties of modern Arabic can be divided into several dialect bundles, which in turn contain a large number of dialects. Some of these dialects are so different from one another that, if we use mutual intelligibility as a distinguishing criterion, we should really speak of the modern Arabic *languages*, in plural. Only for cultural reasons, and because these dialects share a literary (and formal spoken) standard, do we usually find the term “dialect” used for the diverse forms of modern Arabic. Thus all Arabic speakers share a common written language, though their vernacular tongues can differ considerably.

Scholars usually divide the modern dialects into five major groups: Arabian peninsular, Mesopotamian, Syro-Palestinian (or Syro-Lebanese), Egyptian, and Maghrebi (or North African). This division is largely geographic, though there are indeed linguistic characteristics that pertain to each group. The individual dialects within each of these groups can vary considerably, not only with respect to location, but often also with respect to religious affiliation. For example, one cannot speak accurately of Baghdadi Arabic, but only of Muslim, Jewish, or Christian Baghdadi Arabic (Blanc 1964). There is also often a difference between the Arabic of the Bedouin (nomads) and that of sedentary Arabic speakers in the same region. Linguistic subgrouping of the Arabic dialects is an enormously difficult task and so scholars have for the most part remained satisfied with this rough geographical division.

One variety of modern Arabic stands apart from the rest, in that it can safely be designated as a separate language. This is Maltese, spoken on Malta and its neighboring islands. Maltese has no tradition of written Arabic (in either its classical or modern standardized form), and instead has developed a written tradition of its own, using the Roman script. But historically, Maltese can be classified as a Maghrebi Arabic dialect, and despite the many phonological and lexical influences of Romance languages (and more recently, English), it is still easily recognizable as such.

Finally, it should be mentioned that there exist in Africa some creolized varieties of Arabic, notably Juba Arabic in southern Sudan and the closely related Nubi (or Ki-Nubi) in Uganda and Kenya. These are well known among creole specialists, but little studied by Semitists.

1.6 Ṣayhadic (Old South Arabian)

The Ṣayhadic group—also called Old South Arabian, Ancient South Arabian, or Epigraphic South Arabian—includes four languages (or dialects): Sabaic (or Sabean), Minaic (or Minean), Qatabanic (or Qatabanian), and Ḥaḍramitic. These designations are based on those used by the Greek scholar Eratosthenes in his *Geography* (late 3rd century BCE) for the four main peoples who inhabited the area of Southern Arabia corresponding roughly to what is now Yemen (see the edition of Roller 2010). The term Ṣayhadic derives from Ṣayhad, the name that medieval Arabic geographers gave to the Yemeni desert area now called Ramlat as-Sabʿatayn, at the fringe of which the speakers of these languages had their major cities. Ṣayhadic is not yet a widely used term, but it is preferable to the other possibilities, since it avoids any misleading connections with the terms Arabic, Ancient North Arabian (§1.5), and Modern South Arabian (§1.3). It also allows the possibility of distinguishing Sabaic, Minaic, Qatabanic, and Ḥaḍramitic from the rare and very poorly understood other epigraphic languages that seem to have existed in ancient South Arabia (Beeston 1984; 1987). The approximate dates of written attestation for the Ṣayhadic languages are as follows:

Sabaic	(*ca.* 1000 BCE–*ca.* 560 CE)
Minaic	(*ca.* 1000 BCE–*ca.* 120 BCE)
Qatabanic	(*ca.* 700 BCE–*ca.* 200 CE)
Ḥaḍramitic	(*ca.* 700 BCE–*ca.* 300 CE)

The Ṣayhadic languages are known almost exclusively from monumental texts, found mainly in modern Yemen and Saudi Arabia, but also in Ethiopia and Northern Arabia (e.g., Jordan, Syria, and Iraq). There are several thousands of these, though the great majority are in Sabaic. As can be seen from the list of dates above, Sabaic also has the longest period of attestation, and can be divided into different dialects (Stein 2004). Ḥaḍramitic is the most poorly attested. The limited content of these monumental texts, the almost complete lack of vocalization in the script, and the paucity of material for some of the languages mean that many features of the languages remain unknown. Enough is known, however, to allow for a reasonably certain classification of their position within the Semitic family.

The Ṣayhadic monumental texts are written in a distinctive consonantal alphabet that is distantly related to, but very different looking from, the Hebrew and Aramaic alphabets. This alphabet was borrowed by the Ethiopians, and survives in the modern Ethiopian script (see above, §1.4).

Since the 1970s, several thousand texts of a different type have been discovered, namely texts written in a cursive script on small wooden sticks and palm-leaf stalks. Unlike the monumental inscriptions, these texts seem to represent a more "everyday" type of writing, including personal letters and economic documents. Until the publication of Stein (2010), only a few dozen of these texts had been published. The unclear script and sometimes unknown vocabulary of these texts, along with their often poor state of preservation, can make them very difficult to read and interpret. Still, they have added to our understanding of the Ṣayhadic languages.

There is evidence from the comments of Arabic authors that Sabaic continued to be spoken into medieval times. Some have suggested the possibility that a variety of Ṣayhadic (presumably Sabaic) is still spoken in a small pocket of northwestern Yemen, but this seems very unlikely (Watson et al. 2006). It is surely the case, however, that Ṣayhadic has exerted influence on many of the Yemeni dialects of Arabic.

1.7 UGARITIC

Ugaritic is the language that was spoken around ancient Ugarit (now called Ras Shamra), a city located just a few miles north of modern Latakia, on the Syrian coast of the Mediterranean. Texts are attested only for a short period in history, from about 1380 to 1180 BCE. Ugaritic was discovered by modern scholars only in 1928. About 1500 texts are known, most of which are very short. These are written in a unique cuneiform script that looks superficially like logo-syllabic cuneiform systems (e.g., Akkadian), but in fact is an alphabet of about thirty characters. Some Ugaritic is also attested in Akkadian syllabic cuneiform, which, since the Ugaritic alphabet rarely indicates vowels, provides important evidence for the vocalization of the language.

The Ugaritic texts cover a wide variety of genres, including epic poems, religious texts, letters, divination texts, and school texts, among others. It is most widely studied by biblical scholars, who have noted many similarities between Ugaritic literature and biblical literature, and who have used this language to shed light on difficult Hebrew words and forms. As one of the earliest attested forms of Northwest Semitic, it is of importance not only to the study of the Hebrew Bible, but also to the study of Semitic in general.

1.8 CANAANITE

The most prominent member of the Canaanite branch of the Semitic family is Hebrew. In the ancient period, our main source of Hebrew comes from the Hebrew Bible (or Old Testament), which includes material that was written during the period of (roughly) 1150–150 BCE. However, the earliest biblical manuscripts that are extant today date from only about 100 BCE (from among the Dead Sea Scrolls); the oldest complete Hebrew Bible dates from only around 1000 CE. From the biblical period, a number of Hebrew inscriptions are known, some from as early as the 10th century BCE, though few are of any significant length. Given that the Hebrew Bible contains material written over the span of a millennium, it is not surprising that one finds differences in the language of the biblical books. Thus, for example, scholars distinguish between Standard Biblical Hebrew and Late Biblical Hebrew, with the dividing point at around 550 BCE. There is also evidence of synchronic dialectal variation, with Standard Biblical Hebrew reflecting the dialect of Judah in general, and with some portions of the Bible reflecting a northern dialect, termed Israelian Hebrew by scholars (Rendsburg 2003a). Still, Biblical Hebrew is overall relatively uniform.

From the post-biblical period comes Qumran Hebrew, which is the language of the non-biblical texts among the Dead Sea Scrolls, dated mainly to the 2nd and 1st centuries BCE. Qumran Hebrew continues Late Biblical Hebrew, though it also exhibits a few linguistic peculiarities unknown from any other variety of Hebrew.

From the 2nd and 3rd centuries CE, we find a dialect of Hebrew that is usually called Rabbinic or Mishnaic Hebrew. In this dialect, we have several important Jewish texts, the most prominent of which is the Mishnah. Rabbinic Hebrew is distinct in many ways from both Biblical Hebrew and Qumran Hebrew, and seems to stem from a northern (Galilean) dialect (Rendsburg 2003b).

Hebrew died out as spoken language by about the 3rd century CE, but remained in use as a literary and liturgical language among Jews. In this capacity, we find writers imitating both the Biblical and Rabbinic types of Hebrew. Though the language was not anyone's native tongue, it continued to develop throughout the Middle Ages, as new vocabulary was invented or borrowed as needed. There is an enormous corpus of medieval Hebrew works, representing a wide variety of genres, much of it still unpublished.

In the late 18th and early 19th centuries, Hebrew began the road to modernization, and from this period we find many original secular works, such as plays, novels, and newspapers. In the late 19th century there began a movement to revive Hebrew as a spoken language, coinciding with the Zionist movement to reclaim Israel as the Jewish homeland. This unprecedented revival led to the creation of Modern Hebrew (or Israeli Hebrew), which is today the official language of Israel, and is spoken by about six million Israelis. The grammar of the modern language is based heavily on Biblical Hebrew, with many elements from Hebrew of later periods, as well as a large number of newly created and borrowed words.

Hebrew is the only Canaanite language still in use, but there are several others known from the ancient period, the most notable of which is Phoenician. Phoenician is the name that was used by the ancient Greeks to describe the Canaanite peoples who inhabited the coastal plain of what is now Lebanon and northern Israel. The Phoenician language is attested in inscriptions beginning in about 1000 BCE. Because the Phoenicians were seafarers who traveled throughout the Mediterranean, Phoenician inscriptions have been found not only in Lebanon and the vicinity, but also in Cyprus, Greece, Malta, Sicily, Sardinia, Spain, and elsewhere. The dialect of the Phoenician colony that was established at Carthage (near modern Tunis, in Tunisia) is referred to as Punic, which is attested from the 6th century BCE until about the 4th century CE. Inscriptions from after the fall of Carthage (146 BCE) are usually referred to as Neo-Punic or Late Punic. Most Phoenician, including Punic, is written in an alphabet very close to that of ancient Hebrew, but in the latest period we also find inscriptions in Latin or Greek characters.

In addition to Hebrew and Phoenician, there were several other ancient Canaanite dialects, including Moabite, Edomite, and Ammonite. Our knowledge of these dialects comes from a relatively small number of inscriptions from the first millennium BCE, found in what is now western Jordan and Israel. The longest inscription, by far, is a Moabite text of about thirty-five lines from the 9th century BCE, known as the Mesha Stele, since it concerns King Mesha of Moab. The remaining inscriptions are all short and fragmentary, and sometimes it is impossible to determine which dialect is attested in a given inscription. Knowledge of these few Canaanite dialects remains rather poor.

In the late 19th century, an archive of several hundred cuneiform tablets was discovered at Tell El-Amarna in Egypt, about 200 miles south of Cairo. This archive dates from about 1350 BCE, and represents the diplomatic correspondence between Egypt and its vassal states in the Levant, as well as with other powers, like the Babylonians and the Hittites. The correspondence was mainly in Akkadian, since, as noted above (§1.1), Akkadian was the *lingua franca* of the Near East at this time. However, the letters that originated in the various Canaanite cities (in what is now Israel and Lebanon) were often written in very poor Akkadian, with numerous Canaanite words, and even Canaanite grammatical forms and word order. So while the language of the texts is technically Akkadian, many of the Amarna letters provide evidence of Canaanite grammar and vocabulary. And since this corpus pre-dates the attestation of Hebrew or Phoenician by several hundred years, it is an important source for the study of early Canaanite.

1.9 ARAMAIC

Aramaic is first attested from about 900 BCE, around the same time as Hebrew. This makes Aramaic and Hebrew the Semitic languages with the longest attested histories (about three thousand years). Yet unlike Hebrew, Aramaic has never ceased to be a living, spoken language. During the nearly three millennia of its attestation, Aramaic can be divided into a large number of dialects, both chronologically and geographically. There are various schemes for dividing Aramaic into chronological periods, but a widely accepted one is the following:

Old Aramaic	(*ca.* 900–700 BCE)
Imperial Aramaic	(*ca.* 700–200 BCE)
Middle Aramaic	(*ca.* 200 BCE–200 CE)
Late Aramaic	(*ca.* 200–700 CE)
Neo-Aramaic (or Modern Aramaic)	(until the present)

As an emendation to this popular scheme, it is useful and more accurate to divide the Imperial Aramaic period into two: Early Imperial Aramaic (*ca.* 700–550 BCE) and Imperial Aramaic (*ca.* 550–200 BCE). Imperial Aramaic (also called Official, Classical, Standard, or Achaemenid Aramaic) became the *lingua franca* of the Near East (promoted by the Assyrian, Babylonian, and Persian empires), and remained widespread even during the Hellenistic and Roman periods. Use of Aramaic began to decline only with the spread of Islam in the 7th century CE.

Discussion of Aramaic dialects can often be confused by the fact that there are several terms that refer to corpora containing more than one Aramaic dialect (e.g., Biblical Aramaic, Targumic Aramaic, Talmudic Aramaic, and Qumran Aramaic), as well as terms which refer to a corpus within a dialect (e.g., Egyptian Aramaic within Imperial Aramaic). For example, Biblical Aramaic refers to the Aramaic of the books of Ezra and Daniel (as well as a handful of words elsewhere in the Bible). Yet the Aramaic of Ezra is a type of Imperial Aramaic (dating from the 5th century BCE), while that of Daniel is a type of Middle Aramaic (dating from the 2nd century BCE).

Already in the Old Aramaic period there is evidence of geographic dialect differences, but it is not until the end of the Middle Aramaic period that such differences fully manifest themselves in the records. At this time, a clear distinction between western (Palestinian and Nabatean) and eastern (Syrian and Mesopotamian) dialects becomes evident.

By the Late Aramaic period several very important Aramaic literary traditions developed, and the dialect differences become even more apparent. Syriac, originally the dialect of Edessa (now Şanlıurfa [or Urfa], in southeastern Turkey), became the main liturgical language of Christianity in the Fertile Crescent, and is by far the best-attested Aramaic dialect. To the west we find Jewish Palestinian Aramaic (the language of the Palestinian Talmud and Targums), Christian Palestinian Aramaic, and Samaritan Aramaic. To the east of Syriac territory are found the closely related Jewish Babylonian Aramaic (the language of the Babylonian Talmud) and Mandaic. Syriac remains a liturgical language among some eastern churches. The various Jewish dialects of Aramaic continue to be widely read by learned Jews, thanks to its use in the biblical books of Ezra and Daniel, the two Talmuds, and several other compositions important to the Jewish religion.

The Aramaic language has developed into a number of modern dialects, collectively known as Neo-Aramaic. Many of these Neo-Aramaic dialects are unquestionably distinct enough to be called languages. Neo-Aramaic has traditionally been spoken in a noncontiguous area covering parts of Syria, southeastern Turkey, northern Iraq, and northwestern and southwestern Iran, mainly by Jewish and Christian communities. However, as a result of the great political upheavals of the 20th century (most notably, World War I, the establishment of the State of Israel, and the aggression of Saddam Hussein), many, if not most, Neo-Aramaic speakers have been displaced from these areas. Nearly all Jewish Neo-Aramaic speakers have moved to Israel or the United States since 1948, and many Christians have also emigrated (to the United States, Europe, or Australia), or at least have moved to larger, Arabic-speaking cities.

The split between eastern and western dialects that is seen already in the Middle and Late Aramaic periods has survived into the present, though none of the modern languages is the direct descendent of any recorded ancient dialect. In the modern remnant of the western branch, known as Western Neo-Aramaic, there survive only three closely related dialects, spoken in the Syrian villages of Ma‘lula, Bax‘a, and Jubb‘adin, located about thirty-five miles northeast of Damascus. The rest of the modern languages, those of the Eastern Neo-Aramaic branch, can be further divided into three subgroups: Central Eastern Neo-Aramaic (CENA), Northeastern Neo-Aramaic (NENA), and Neo-Mandaic.

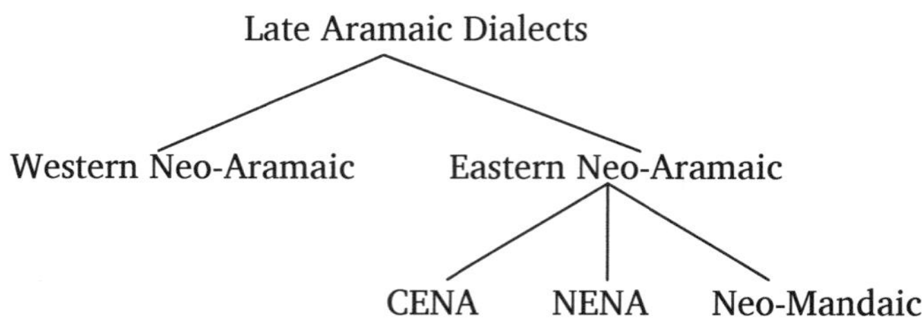

The Central Eastern Neo-Aramaic branch includes just Ṭuroyo and the closely related, but nearly extinct, dialect of Mlaḥso. Ṭuroyo is one of the most thriving of the Neo-Aramaic languages, both in its native territory (the Tur Abdin region of southeastern Turkey) and abroad. In Sweden and in Germany, a handful of books in Turoyo have been published in recent years (in both Roman and Syriac scripts). Neo-Mandaic is the highly endangered, modern reflex of Mandaic, the language of the Mandean religion and its followers. Its speakers, living mainly in Iran, number only in the low hundreds.

The Northeastern Neo-Aramaic subgroup includes approximately 150 different dialects, many of which are mutually unintelligible. They are traditionally spoken in the loosely-defined region known as Kurdistan. A number of the NENA dialects have been well studied in recent years, but many more have yet to be investigated fully. One interesting fact about the NENA languages is that dialect grouping is in many cases based on religious affiliation, rather than geographic location. So, for example, the Jewish Neo-Aramaic dialect of one town may be incomprehensible to the Christian Neo-Aramaic speakers of the same town, but not to Jewish speakers of another village. Such a state of affairs is somewhat analogous to the situation of African American Vernacular English, which defies the traditional geographical dialect boundaries of the United States. The Neo-Aramaic languages, in particular those of the NENA group, have been heavily influenced by neighboring non-Semitic languages (especially Kurdish and Turkish), and therefore are in many ways quite divergent from classical varieties of Aramaic.

2 PHONOLOGY

2.1 SEMITIC CONSONANTS

Proto-Semitic had the following consonant phonemes, according to the most recent scholarship (Huehnergard 2004):

		Labial	Inter-dental	Dental/ Alveolar	Palatal	Velar	Pharyngeal	Glottal
Stops:	voiceless	*p*		*t*		*k*		*ʔ*
	voiced	*b*		*d*		*g*		
	glottalic			*t'*		*k'*		
Affricates:	voiceless			*^{t}s*				
	voiced			*^{d}z*				
	glottalic			*$^{t}s'$*				
Fricatives:	voiceless		*θ*	*s*		*x*	*ħ*	*h*
	voiced		*ð*			*ɣ*	*ʕ*	
	glottalic		*θ'*			*(x')*		
Lateral continuants:								
	voiceless			*ɬ*				
	voiced			*l*				
	glottalic			*ɬ'*				
Nasals		*m*		*n*				
Glides		*w*			*y*			
Tap/Trill				*r*				

It is noteworthy that among the series of interdental fricatives, dental/alveolar stops, dental/alveolar affricates, dental/alveolar lateral continuants, and velar stops, there is a three-way contrast: voiceless, voiced, and glottalic. The glottalic consonants are often referred to in Semitic scholarly literature as "emphatic", a rather vague term. In Arabic, these consonants are either velarized or pharyngealized (except **k'*, which in Classical and Modern Standard Arabic is realized as a voiceless uvular stop *q*), while in Ethiopian and Modern South Arabian, they remained glottalic (ejective). It is, of course, difficult to know how they were pronounced in the ancient languages (Akkadian, Biblical Hebrew, Sabaic, etc.), but there is good evidence that the glottalic pronunciation can be reconstructed for Proto-Semitic and Akkadian (Aro 1977; Zemánek 1996; Kouwenberg 2003). For this reason, the transcriptions indicating a following glottal stop (e.g., *t'*) are preferable to the more traditional dotted letters (e.g., *ṭ*) for Proto-Semitic, Akkadian, Ethiopian, and Modern South Arabian. A three-way contrast likely also existed among the velar fricatives, though the reconstructed consonant **x'* has not yet been widely accepted. It was first proposed by Huehnergard (2003), on the basis of the standard comparative method. It survives in none of the attested languages; in East Semitic it has merged with **x*, while in all of West Semitic it has merged with **ħ*. In Tigrinya, *x'* is found as a fricativized allophone of *k'*, unconnected with Proto-Semitic **x'*. There is no evidence for a Proto-Semitic glottalic labial *p'*, though this phoneme exists in Ethiopian languages. Most Ethiopian words with *p'* are borrowings from Greek or other languages (e.g., Geʿez *p'ant'ak'ost'e* 'Pentecost').

The affricate set **ᵗs*, **ᵈz*, **ᵗs'* has traditionally been reconstructed as **s*, **z*, **ṣ*, but there is compelling evidence to suggest that these phonemes were in fact affricates. It is equally likely that the consonant traditionally reconstructed as palatal **š* was really dental/alveolar **s* (Faber 1981; 1985). The affricates were deaffricated in much of the Semitic family (e.g., Arabic and Ethiopian), while Proto-Semitic **s* shifted to *š* in a number of the languages (e.g., Biblical Hebrew and Babylonian Akkadian).

The phoneme **ɬ* (usually transcribed *ś* by Semitists) is distinct in a number of the ancient languages (e.g., Biblical Hebrew, Old and Imperial Aramaic, Ṣayhadic, and Geʿez), and there is solid evidence for its pronunciation as a lateral continuant (Steiner 1977). Among the modern languages, *ɬ* survives only among the Modern South Arabian group. In some languages, like Hebrew and Aramaic, **ɬ* came to be pronounced *s*, while in Arabic it developed into the phoneme *š*. The glottalic lateral *ɬ'* likewise survives only among the Modern South Arabian group. In Arabic it became a velarized or pharyngealized *d*, i.e., [$d^ɣ$] or [$d^ʕ$] (usually transcribed *ḍ*), while in Hebrew and Akkadian it merged with **ᵗs'*. In Old Aramaic, it became a sound that was written with the same symbol used for *k'* (though the phonemes did not merge), but in later Aramaic it merged with ʕ.

The phoneme **p* became a fricative *f* in the Arabic, Old South Arabian, Modern South Arabian, and Ethiopian groups, that is, all of the more southerly Semitic languages. This is one of the features that led early Semitists to classify these languages together in a subgroup called "South Semitic". Such a simple phonetic change is, of course, of no value in classification. In fact, the shift **p* > *f* is just an areal phenomenon, one of several that are common to these languages. In the Ethiopian languages, a phoneme *p* has been re-introduced; like *p'*, it is found mainly in loanwords from European languages (e.g., Amharic *polis* 'police; policeman').

In most Ethiopian Semitic languages, there also exists a series of labio-velar consonants. For example, in Geʿez we find the phonemes k^w, k'^w, g^w, and x^w. In some cases, it is clear that the labio-velar element derives from the historical presence of the vowel **u*, e.g., *kʷəll-* 'all' < **kull-*. In other cases, there is no obvious explanation for the presence of the labio-velar element.

Examples of palatalization within the various Semitic languages are numerous. For example, in most modern Arabic dialects, the Proto-Semitic phoneme **g* is realized as some sort of palatal, most often as *j*, *ž*, g^y, or *y* (that is, [dʒ], [ʒ], [g^y], or [j]). The phoneme **k* is also palatalized to *č* (that is, [tʃ]) in a few Arabic dialects, including Iraqi dialects. Palatalization of *t*, *k*, and *g* is also known from some Neo-Aramaic dialects. But palatalization is most widespread in the South Ethiopian Semitic languages, where palatalization has also resulted in additional phonemes. For example, Amharic has acquired the palatal phonemes *č*, *č'*, *j*, *ɲ*, *š*, and *ž*, which also occur as allophones of the dentals *t*, *t'*, *d*, *n*, *s*, and *z*, respectively. Likewise, the inherited Amharic palatal phoneme *y* is also an allophone of *l*.

Some have suggested reconstructing the syllabic sonorants **l̩*, **m̩*, and **n̩* for Proto-Semitic, in order to explain some seemingly irregular correspondences among the descendent languages (Testen 1985; 1993; 1995). How these syllabics would have fit into the phonological system of Proto-Semitic is unclear, as are their implications for Proto-Semitic syllable structure. Despite strong evidence for reconstructioning these syllabics, they remain somewhat controversial.

2.2 Semitic Vowels

The vowel system reconstructed for Proto-Semitic is quite simple. There were three vowels, **a*, **i*, and **u*, and each of these could occur either short or long.

Short:	i	a	u
Long:	ī	ā	ū

This system is preserved in Classical Arabic, while most other ancient and modern languages exhibit developments in their vowel systems. Of course, for many of the ancient languages whose writing systems are purely consonantal (e.g., Phoenician and Sabaic), our knowledge of their vowel systems is quite limited.

Vowels play an essential part in the case system of Semitic (§3.2.2). For singular nouns and internal plurals (§3.2.1), for example, the case endings in Proto-Semitic were simply the short vowels: *-u* for nominative, *-a* for accusative, and *-i* for genitive. Simple sound change led to the deterioration of case endings in many of the languages. For example, in Proto-Hebrew, final short vowels were lost, leading to the complete loss of the case system. In Ge'ez, the short vowels **u* and **i* merged to *ə* in all positions, leading to a merger of the nominative and genitive cases.

2.3 Roots and Root Integrity

Perhaps the most characteristic feature of the Semitic languages, is the system of consonantal roots, which has had great effect in the area of phonology. The concept of the consonantal root is fundamental to the morphology and lexicon of Semitic, and is in fact a defining characteristic of the family. All verbs and the majority of nouns possess a set of root consonants, usually three, which are used in conjunction with vocalic templates to form words. These templates, which cause the interlacing of the consonants with vowels and often include the addition of prefixes or suffixes, are used to form all words in the language, save the pronouns and various kinds of particles. The roots carry the lexical meanings, while the templates carry the grammatical functions. For example, the Arabic root *RKB* has a meaning associated with the act of riding, as seen in the words *rakiba* 'he rode', *yarkabu* 'he rides', *rākibun* 'a rider (NOM.)', *rakkābun* 'a (professional) horseman (NOM.)', *markabatun* 'vehicle; carriage (NOM.)', and *murakkabun* 'mounted (NOM.)'. In each of these words, the root appears with a particular set of vowels, along with a prefix and/or a suffix.

The Semitic roots, as a system, are closely tied in with the study of phonology. This is because there is a set of constraints on which consonants can co-occur within a triliteral root, at least in Proto-Semitic (Greenberg 1950). For example, the first and second root consonants cannot be identical, and homorganic consonants (that is, consonants which share their point of articulation), rarely co-occur within a root. These phonological restrictions thus limit the number of possible Semitic roots.

The root system has also had a great effect on the phonologies of the Semitic languages through the principle of root integrity (Huehnergard 2004). According to this principle, the triliteral root should remain intact, even at the expense of regular sound changes. For example, in Ge'ez we find the verbs *k'ʷarra* 'be cold', causative *ʔak'ʷrara* 'cool'. It was already noted above that the Ethiopian labio-velars normally derive from the historical presence of the vowel **u*. In these verb forms, there is no historical reason to assume the presence of a labio-velar. However, the related nouns *k'ʷərr* and *k'ʷərrat*, both meaning 'cold', derive from **k'urr* and **k'urrat*, respectively. By regular sound change, we would expect to find the nouns *k'ʷərr* and *k'ʷərrat*, and the verbs ***k'arra* 'be cold' and ***ʔak'rara*, but the pressure to maintain root integrity has led to the spread of the labio-velar (which is a separate phoneme) to all words containing this root.

Another example of root integrity pertains to a more widespread sound change. In Proto-West Semitic, there seems to have been a sound rule by which **s* became **h* before vowels (Voigt 1987). By such a change, a verb form such as **samiʕa* 'he heard' would have become ***hamiʕa*, while a verb form such as **yismaʕu* 'he hears' would have remained unchanged. This alternation of root consonants was deemed unacceptable, as a violation of root integrity, with the result that the sound change of **s* > **h* was blocked in all verbal roots. We thus see evidence of this sound change only in words not associated with a root: the third person pronouns (e.g., Akkadian *šū* ~ Hebrew *hū*), the prefix of the causative verbal stem (e.g., Akkadian *š-* ~ Hebrew *h-*), the conditional particle (e.g., Akkadian *šumma* ~ Ugaritic *hm*), and a few others. Another change of **s* > **h* took place in the history of the Modern South Arabian languages (cf. Mehri *hūma* 'he heard'), but this is separate from, and later than, the sound change that was common to West Semitic.

3 MORPHOLOGY

3.1 PRONOUNS

3.1.1 INDEPENDENT PRONOUNS

All Semitic languages have a set of independent pronouns, that is, pronouns consisting of an independent (non-clitic) morpheme. Proto-Semitic distinguished the following forms (Huehnergard 2004):

<table>
<tr><th></th><th>SG</th><th>DU</th><th>PL</th></tr>
<tr><td>1st C</td><td>ʔana / ʔanāku</td><td>(none?)</td><td>niħnu</td></tr>
<tr><td>2nd M</td><td>ʔanta</td><td rowspan="2">ʔantumā</td><td>ʔantum</td></tr>
<tr><td>2nd F</td><td>ʔanti</td><td>ʔantin</td></tr>
<tr><td>3rd M</td><td>suʔa</td><td rowspan="2">sumā</td><td>sum</td></tr>
<tr><td>3rd F</td><td>siʔa</td><td>sin</td></tr>
</table>

Gender was distinguished for second and third persons only, hence the designation "common" for the first person pronouns. This lack of gender distinction in the first person forms applies to the verbal system as well. The two first person singular pronouns reconstructed for Proto-Semitic seem to have been free variants, as they are in some of the languages (e.g., Hebrew). A first person dual independent pronoun is attested only in the Modern South Arabian languages (e.g., Omani Mehri *əkay*), and so there is little evidence on which to base a Proto-Semitic reconstruction (E. Wagner 1952). All of the Proto-Semitic first and second person forms, with the exception of the first person common plural, seem to be made up of an element *ʔan-* plus a pronominal marker. The origin of the initial element is unknown, though it has parallels elsewhere in Afroasiatic (e.g., in Egyptian).

The independent pronouns can serve as subjects of verbless (copular) clauses, as in (1), or they can provide emphasis or topicalization in a verbal clause, as in (2).

Biblical Hebrew

(1) *mē-ʔayin ʔattem*
from-where 2M.PL
'Where are you from?' (Gen. 29:4)

(2) *wə-ʔattem pərū*
CONJ-2M.PL be.fruitful:IMPER.M.PL
ū-rəbū
CONJ-multiply:IMPER.M.PL
'And you, be fruitful and multiply.' (Gen. 9:7)

In the attested Semitic languages, even in many of the ancient ones, the inherited set of independent pronouns has usually been reduced to include fewer forms. Loss of the dual is very common, and loss of gender distinction is also found in some languages, to varying degrees. For example, in the Northeastern Neo-Aramaic (NENA) Jewish dialect of Arbel (northern Iraq), gender is distinguished only for the second person singular forms, and even then only optionally (Khan 1999). In Maltese, gender is distinguished only in the third person singular forms.

NENA (Arbel)

	SG	PL
1st C	*ʔāna*	*ʔatxan/ʔaxnan*
2nd M	*ʔat / ʔāti*	*ʔatxun*
2nd F	*ʔat*	
3rd C	*ʔo*	*ʔoni*

Maltese

	SG	PL
1st C	*jien(a)*	*aħna*
2nd C	*int(i)*	*intom*
3rd M	*hu(wa)*	*huma*
3rd F	*hi(ja)*	

No independent objective pronouns can be reconstructed for Proto-Semitic—at least not for the first and second persons—but a number of languages have developed independent accusative and dative pronouns. Hebrew, for example, has a set of direct object pronouns based on the particle *ʔēt* (< **ʔiyyāt*), which on its own marks definite direct objects.

Biblical Hebrew

	SG	PL
1st C	*ʔōti*	*ʔōtānū*
2nd M	*ʔōtəkā*	*ʔetkem*
2nd F	*ʔōtāk*	*ʔetken*
3rd M	*ʔōtō*	*ʔōtām (ʔethem)*
3rd F	*ʔōtāh*	*ʔethen (ʔōtān)*

Similar direct object pronouns based on an original morpheme **ʔiyyāt* are attested in Aramaic, Arabic, and Modern South Arabian (Rubin 2005). Different sources are found in other languages, for example, the Geʿez independent direct object pronoun is based on a stem *kiyā-*, of unclear origin.

The Proto-Semitic third person pronouns, originally anaphoric pronouns, probably had an oblique (objective) case with suffixed *-ti*. This element is found in the oblique forms of the third person pronouns in Ugaritic (e.g., **huwa* 'he', oblique **huwāti* 'him'), while in Akkadian this suffix has spread to all persons, resulting in a new set of independent direct object pronouns based on the suffixed pronouns plus the element *-ti* (e.g., *yâti* 'me' < suffixed pronoun *-ya* + *-ti*).

Independent possessive pronouns and possessive adjectives are also not reconstructable for Proto-Semitic, but are found in many Semitic languages. These are most often formed by attaching the suffixed pronouns (§3.1.2) to a genitive exponent, the origin of which can be a relative pronoun or a noun. Examples are Post-Biblical Hebrew *šel* 'of' < relative *še-* + *l-* 'to', and Yemeni Arabic *ħagg* 'of' < Classical Arabic *ħaqq* 'property' (Rubin 2004b; 2005). So from these genitive exponents, we find Modern Hebrew *šeli* 'my; mine' (lit. 'of-me'), *šelxā* 'your; yours' (lit. 'of-you'), etc., and Yemeni Arabic *ħaggī* 'my; mine' (lit. 'of-me'), *ħaggak* 'your; yours' (lit. 'of-you'), etc. In some languages we find independent possessive pronouns and adjectives based on the genitive exponent (stemming from a relative pronoun) plus the independent subject pronouns, as in Amharic *yäne* 'my; mine' (< *yä-* + *ənē*, lit. 'of-I') and Soqoṭri *di-hoh* 'my; mine' (lit. 'of-I').

3.1.2 SUFFIXED PRONOUNS

The Semitic languages also possess a set of suffixed pronouns, used to indicate pronominal possession on nouns (3), pronominal objects of verbs (4), and pronominal objects of prepositions (5) and other particles (6). The forms of the pronouns can vary slightly with the different uses. For example, in Iraqi Arabic, the first person singular suffixed pronoun has the form *-i* after nouns and particles ending in a consonant, *-ya* after nouns and particles ending in a vowel, and *-ni* after verbs, while the third feminine singular pronoun has the form *-ha* in all environments.

Iraqi (Muslim Baghdadi) Arabic

(3) *bēt,* *bēt-i,* *bēt-ak,* *bēt-ha*
house, house-1SG, house-2M.SG, house-3F.SG
'house, my house, your (m.) house, her house'

(4) *šāf,* *šāf-ni,* *šāf-ha*
see:PAST.3M.SG, see:PAST.3M.SG-1SG, see:PAST.3M.SG-3F.SG
'he saw, he saw me, he saw her'

(5) *wara,* *warā-ya,* *warā-k,* *warā-ha*
behind, behind-1SG, behind-2M.SG, behind-3F.SG
'behind, behind me, behind you (m.), behind her'

(6) *wēn,* *wēn-ha,* *wēn-hum*
where, where-3F.SG, where-3M.PL
'where? where is she? where are they?' (Erwin 1963)

In the Central Semitic languages, the definite article and a possessive pronominal suffix cannot co-occur. This is probably because nouns with a possessive pronominal suffix are already treated as definite for the purposes of agreement. The opposite is true for Omani Mehri, in which we find the possessive suffixes attached to the definite form of the noun (7).

Omani Mehri

(7) *a-bayt-i,* *a-ɣā-k,* *ḥə-brɔ́t-həm*
the-house-1SG, the-brother-2M.SG, the-daughter-3M.PL
'my house, your brother, their daughter' (Rubin 2010b)

3.1.3 REFLEXIVE AND RECIPROCAL PRONOUNS

In the Semitic languages, reflexivity can often be expressed by means of a derived verbal stem (§3.4.1), as in Mehri *šək'rū* 'hide oneself' (vs. *k'ərū* 'hide, conceal'), Ge'ez *taxabʔa* 'hide oneself' (vs. *xabʔa* 'hide, conceal'), and Arabic *ʔixtafā* 'hide oneself' (vs. *ʔaxfā* 'hide, conceal'). However, most Semitic languages have developed a means of expressing an independent reflexive pronoun. This is nearly always the result of a grammaticalization based on a word meaning 'body' or a part of the body, such as 'head', 'soul', 'eye', or 'bone' (Rubin 2005). Some examples are Post-Biblical Hebrew *ʕaṣm-* (< *ʕéṣem* 'bone'), Amharic *ras-* (< 'head') (8), Wolane *gäg-* (< 'body'), Old Assyrian *pagr-* (< 'body'), Classical Arabic *nafs-* (< 'soul') (9) and *ʕayn-* (< 'eye'), and Algerian Arabic *rōḥ-* (< 'soul, spirit, breath'). Only in a couple of cases is the origin of a reflexive pronoun unknown, as with Akkadian *ramān-*.

Amharic

(8) *ras-u-n* *gäddälä*
head-3M.SG-ACC kill:PAST.3M.SG
'He killed himself.' (Leslau 1995)

Classical Arabic

(9) *qāla* *li-nafs-i-hī*
say:PAST.3M.SG to-soul-GEN-3M.SG
'he said to himself' (Fischer 2002)

Likewise, reciprocity can be expressed by means of a verbal stem (e.g., Modern Hebrew *hitkatev* 'correspond' vs. *katav* 'write'; Mehri *ɣatrəb* 'know one another' vs. *ɣərūb* 'know'), but many languages have also developed a grammaticalized reciprocal pronoun. Examples are Syriac *ħdāde* 'each other' (< *ħad* 'one'), Mehri *t'āt'īday-* 'each other' (< *t'ād* 'one'), Wolane *gäg bä-gäg* 'each other' (< *gäg* 'body'), and Akkadian *axāmiš* or *axāʔiš* 'each other' (< *axu* 'brother').

3.2 NOMINAL SYSTEM

3.2.1 GENDER AND NUMBER

The Semitic nominal system (including both nouns and adjectives) distinguishes two genders, masculine and feminine. Feminine nouns are normally predictable from the presence of a feminine suffixed morpheme **-(V)t*. As a result of sound change, this feminine suffix can take a variety of shapes in the languages, for example, Hebrew *-ā* (< **-at*), Mehri *-ōt* (< **-at*), and Jewish NENA of Arbel *la* (< **-θ-ā* < **-t-ā*) (the feminine marker also has other allomorphs in these languages). Every language includes a set of feminine nouns, both animate and inanimate, which lack an explicit feminine morpheme, such as Mehri *ħāmē* 'mother', *ʔayn* 'eye', and *ʔārk'ayb* 'mouse'. The word for 'mother' and the words for parts of the body tend to fall in this category. Gender marking on the noun is largely absent from most South Ethiopian languages, though the category of gender is still retained for agreement purposes. In Arabic, which possesses a large number of grammatically singular nouns representing collectives, the feminine form serves to indicate an individual item. For example, in Classical Arabic, we find M. *damʕ* 'tears', F. *damʕa* 'a tear', and M. *tamr* 'dates', F. *tamra* 'a date'.

With regard to number, the Proto-Semitic nominal system distinguished singular, dual, and plural. The dual was lost as a productive feature in many of the languages, including Hebrew, Aramaic, Akkadian (except in the oldest periods), and all of Ethiopian, though in most of these languages there are remnants. For example, in Biblical Hebrew, the inherited dual ending *-ayim* is preserved in the forms of certain numerals, like *štayim* 'two' and *mātayim* 'two hundred'; many of the body parts that occur in pairs, like *ʕēnayim* 'eyes' and *ʔoznayim* 'ears'; certain time words, like *yōmayim* 'two days' and *šənātayim* 'two years'; and words for tools or devices with two parts, like *məṣiltayim* ‘cymbals’ and *melqāḥayim* ‘tongs’. Interestingly, in Modern Hebrew, this dual suffix has become semi-productive again, not in spontaneous speech, but in the conscious creation of new words, such as *mišqafayim* ‘eyeglasses’ and *ʔofanayim* ‘bicycle’. In languages without a productive dual, like Hebrew, nouns with vestigial dual forms are treated as plural for purposes of agreement with verbs and adjectives, e.g., Modern Hebrew *mišqafayim yəqarim* ‘expensive[PL] eyeglasses[DU]’. Languages with a productive dual, like Arabic, have dual forms of verbs and adjectives, as well.

Formation of the Semitic plural is a complex issue. There are two basic ways in which plurality can be indicated. The first is by external means, with the addition of a suffixed morpheme to the noun. The second is by internal means, by replacement of the noun’s vocalic pattern; these are usually termed “internal plurals” or “broken plurals”. In East Semitic (10) and in Northwest Semitic (11), we find only the external means of plural marking, though a few noun types show remnants of internal plural marking (Huehnergard 1987a; 1991). In Arabic (12), Ṣayhadic, Ethiopian, and Modern South Arabian (13), internal plural marking is widespread, though we find external plural marking in these languages as well. In some modern South Ethiopian languages, external plural marking has become more common.

Standard Babylonian Akkadian

(10) *mār-u* ‘son’ (NOM.), PL. *mār-ū* (NOM.)
mārt-u ‘daughter’ (NOM.), PL. *mār-āt-u* (NOM.)

Biblical Hebrew

(11) *gibbōr* ‘warrior’, PL. *gibbōr-īm*
śāpā ‘language’, PL. *śāp-ōt*

Egyptian Arabic

(12) *walad* ‘child’, PL. *awlād*
xādim ‘servant’, PL. *xadam*

Omani Mehri

(13) *ɣayg* ‘man’, PL. *ɣəyōg*
hēxər ‘old man’, PL. *hīxār*

Sometimes both types of plural marking can be used together in the same word, and so we find plural marking that is indicated by both pattern replacement and suffixation; cf. Ge'ez *hagar* 'city', PL. *ʔahgur* (internal) or *ʔahgur-āt* (internal plus external).

In South Ethiopian, we find an innovative type of internal plural that makes use of reduplication. For example, in Zay, in which external plural marking is the norm, and in which other types of internal plural marking have been lost, some nouns indicate plural through partial reduplication, as in *dəha* 'poor, orphan', PL. *dəhāhu*; *gāla* 'camel', PL. *gālālu*; and *č'ik'ile* 'elbow', PL. *č'ik'ilālu* (Leslau 1999).

3.2.2 NOMINAL CASE

Proto-Semitic distinguished three cases: nominative, accusative, and genitive. In addition to indicating a direct object, the accusative case was used in some adverbial constructions (14). The genitive case was used both for genitive constructions (see below, §3.2.3) and to mark the objects of prepositions.

Classical Arabic

(14)	*yasʕā*	*layl-an*	*wa-nahār-an*
	hurry:NONPAST.3M.SG	night-ACC.INDEF	and-day-ACC.INDEF

'He hurries night and day.' (Ryding 2005)

Case marking was done by means of vocalic suffixes on the noun. For singular nouns and internal plurals, the case endings were simply the short vowels: *-u* for nominative, *-a* for accusative, *-i* for genitive. In the dual and plural, there was only a two-way distinction between nominative and oblique cases: *-ā* for nominative dual, *-ay* for oblique dual, *-ū* for nominative plural, and *-ī* for oblique plural. If a noun contains a feminine marking suffix, the case marker follows this suffix, e.g., Akkadian *mārt-u* 'daughter (NOM.)'. A case marker precedes any pronominal suffix (e.g., Arabic *li-bayt-i-hā* to-house-GEN-3F.SG 'to her house'; Ge'ez *hagar-a-ka* city-ACC-2M.SG 'your city (ACC.)'), though in Akkadian, the nominative and accusative (but not genitive) case markers were normally dropped before the possessive suffixes for most singular nouns.

The general tendency towards the loss of word-final vowels led to the disappearance of the case system in most languages. For example, in Proto-Hebrew, final short vowels were lost, leading to the complete loss of the case system in the singular. In the plural, the oblique plural *-ī*, with mimation (see §3.2.3), was generalized, resulting in the external masculine plural *-īm*. In modern Arabic spoken dialects, we find this exact change, with loss of the case system and retention of the oblique external masculine plural. In later Akkadian dialects, loss of final short vowels also led to the decline of the case system; the cases are still used in writing the later dialects, but often indiscriminately or incorrectly. In Geʿez, the short vowels **u* and **i* merged to *ə*, in all positions, leading to a merger of the nominative and genitive cases. Word-final *ə* was subsequently lost, though some modern scholars prefer to retain this in transcription. Therefore, Geʿez distinguishes only an accusative case; cf. *hagar* (< **hagar-ə*) 'city', *hagar-a* 'city (ACC.)'.

A number of Semitic languages have developed new means of indicating the accusative. In Canaanite and some early Aramaic dialects, we find a particle derived from a form **ʔiyyāt* (e.g., Hebrew *ʔēt*, Palestinian Aramaic *yāt*), which marks definite direct objects (15). In a number of other languages, including a number of Aramaic dialects (73, in §4.5), some Arabic dialects (16), Geʿez, Tigrinya (17), and Tigré, the dative preposition has developed into a marker of definite direct objects (Rubin 2005). Amharic marks definite direct objects with a special accusative suffix (8, in §3.1.3), which may also be connected with an earlier dative preposition (Appleyard 2004).

Biblical Hebrew

(15) *bārā* *ʔĕlōhīm* *ʔēt* *haš-šāmayim* *wə-ʔēt*
create:PAST.3M.SG God ACC the-heavens and-ACC
hā-ʔāreṣ
the-earth
'God created the heavens and the earth.' (Gen. 1:1)

Iraqi (Muslim Baghdadi) Arabic

(16) *faṣṣax-a* *l-ir-rādyo*
take.apart:PAST.3M.SG-OBJ.3M.SG DAT-the-radio
'He took apart the radio.' (Erwin 1963)

Tigrinya

(17) *ʔəta* *dəmmu* *n-äti* *s'äba*
that:F.SG cat DAT-that:M.SG milk
sätəyat-o
drink:PAST.3F.SG-OBJ.3M.SG
'The cat drank the milk.' (Melles 2001)

Besides the three basic Proto-Semitic cases discussed above, there are two other suffixes which some scholars have considered to be case endings, namely the suffixes that appear in Akkadian as *-iš* and *-u(m)*. Akkadian *-iš* (< **-is*) is called a terminative-adverbial ending in the standard grammars. It has the basic meaning 'to, for', equivalent to the Akkadian preposition *ana*. It also can be used with adjectives to form adverbs (see §3.5). This suffix likely corresponds to the terminative/directive suffix *-(a)h* found in Hebrew and Ugaritic, e.g., Hebrew *ṣāfōn* 'north', *ṣāfōnāh* 'to the north, northwards'; on the change of *s* > *h* , see §2.3.

The Akkadian suffix *-u(m)* (the final *m* was lost by the end of the Old Babylonian period) functions as a locative-adverbial suffix in Akkadian, e.g., *bīt* 'house', *bītum* 'in the house'. This suffix appears identical in shape to the nominative case ending, though the two behave differently when pronominal suffixes are added. It is unclear, therefore, if the two are historically the same. Some have suggested that this suffix provides evidence of ergativity at some pre-Semitic stage, but this is highly speculative (see Waltisberg 2002 for an argument against ergativity). The locative-adverbial suffix also possibly existed in Ugaritic, though evidence is meager, and there may also be vestiges in other languages (Tropper 2000a).

3.2.3 NOMINAL STATE

Proto-Semitic nouns had two forms, known as "states", the uses of which were connected to a noun's syntactic function. The construct (or bound) state exhibited no special marker (though it retains a case ending in some languages), and was used when the noun governed a directly following element. This element could be a noun in the genitive case, in which case the two elements formed a genitive chain (18); a pronominal (possessive) suffix (19); or a relative clause (20).

Old Babylonian Akkadian

(18) *bēl* *bīt-im*
master:CONSTR house-GEN
'the master of the house'

(19) *bēl-ni*
master:CONSTR-1PL
'our master'

(20) *bīt* *imqut-u*
house:CONSTR fall:PAST.3M.SG-SUBORD
'the house that fell' (von Soden 1995)

When not governing a directly following element, a noun was considered to be in the free (or unbound) state. The free state was marked by a set of nasal suffixes, which appeared after the case endings; the distribution seems to have been **-m* after short vowels and **-na* after long vowels or diphthongs. For example, in Old Babylonian Akkadian, the nominal base *il-* 'god' appears as *ilum* in the nominative singular free form but simply as *il* in the singular construct form (Akkadian singular construct nouns lose case marking); and the nominal base *īn-* 'eye' appears as *īnān* in the nominative dual free form but simply as *īnā* in the nominative dual construct form. We find that most languages have levelled one or the other of the nasal consonants, that is, to **-n* and **-na* (e.g., Arabic) or to **-m* and **-ma* (e.g., Hebrew). The shorter allomorph was lost in many languages, including all of Northwest Semitic, Modern South Arabian, Ethiopian Semitic, most modern Arabic dialects, and later phases of Akkadian. It should be mentioned that the addition of the markers **-n/*-m* and **-na/*-ma* is usually referred to by Semitists as "nunation" and "mimation", after the names of the letters *n* (*nun*) and *m* (*mim*) in the Arabic alphabet.

Although the original function of these allomorphs, **-m* and **-na*, in Proto-Semitic seems to have been to mark the free state, this is not necessarily the case in the daughter languages. For example, in Classical Arabic, these suffixes have become a marker of indefiniteness in the singular (cf. Classical Arabic *wald-u-n* 'a child (NOM.)' vs. *al-wald-u* 'the child (NOM.)'), though the suffixes are dropped when the noun is in the construct state, reflecting their historical function as a marker of the free state only, e.g., *wald-u l-malikat-i* 'the child (NOM.) of the queen'. Since the first member of a genitive chain is syntactically definite, the lack of the suffix *-n* seems to have been reinterpreted as a sign of definiteness in Arabic.

The use of the construct state to express a genitive chain (as in 18, above) and the use of possessive pronominal suffixes with the construct form (as in 19, above) are characteristic features of the Semitic languages. Yet in a number of the languages, one or both of these syntactic features have been lost, or at least have been relegated to less frequent use. As already noted above (§3.1.1), many of the languages have developed independent genitive exponents. The use of the construct state to express a relative clause (as in 20, above) is common only in Akkadian and Ṣayhadic (though not unknown in some other languages, like Biblical Hebrew), and relative clauses are most often expressed with a relative pronoun (see below, §4.10).

Although in Proto-Semitic the free state was the marked form and the construct state was the unmarked form, in a number of languages, as a result of sound change or re-analysis, the construct has become the marked form. For example, in Hebrew, many nouns have a marked construct form that results from the fact that the construct form is regularly unstressed, e.g., *bayit* 'house' (free) < **báyt*, but construct *bēt* < **bayt*. In Geʿez, the construct form of a noun is marked by the suffix *-a*, the origin of which is unclear (Tropper 2000b).

3.2.4 ARTICLES

No definite or indefinite articles can be reconstructed for Proto-Semitic, but articles are found in many of the descendant languages. In Central Semitic, definite articles have developed from demonstratives: Hebrew *ha-* and Arabic *al-* are prefixed to the noun, while Aramaic *-ā* and Sabaic *-(h)n* are suffixed (on the development of the Central Semitic articles, see Rubin 2005). Several modern Semitic languages, including Tigrinya and Turoyo (Neo-Aramaic), also make use of demonstratives to indicate definiteness, and these are on their way to becoming fully functioning definite articles. A number of South Ethiopian languages possess definite articles which derive from third person possessive suffixes, e.g., Amharic *bet-u* 'his house/the house' (Rubin 2010a). This is typologically a more unusual type of grammaticalization, but one that is known from elsewhere (e.g., Indonesian, Yucatec Mayan, and some Turkic languages). Some other Semitic languages have borrowed definite articles, including several NENA dialects, which have borrowed their definite articles from Kurdish, and Omani Mehri, which has likely borrowed its article from surrounding Arabic dialects.

Indefinite articles, where they have evolved, derive from the numeral 'one'. Examples can be found in Neo-Aramaic (21), modern Arabic dialects, and some Ethiopian languages. Occasionaly usage of the numeral 'one' as an indefinite article can also be found in some other languages (e.g., Biblical Hebrew).

NENA (Barwar)
(21) *ʔiθ-wa xa-malka*
EXIST-PAST one-king
'there was a king' (Khan 2008a)

3.3 NUMERALS

In the classical Semitic languages, numerals from 'one' through 'ten' have masculine and feminine forms. Strangely, the masculine numerals from 'three' through 'ten' (that is, those numerals that accompany masculine nouns) look morphologically feminine, while the feminine numerals from 'three' through 'ten' (those numerals that accompany feminine nouns) look morphologically masculine. This peculiar situation has yet to be satisfactorily explained (Hetzron 1967 is one attempt, using Afroasiatic evidence). The table below lists the forms of the numerals 'one' through 'ten' in Classical Arabic (without case endings); note the presence of the feminine morpheme *-at* on the masculine numerals 'three' through 'ten'.

	M	F
1	*wāħid*	*wāħidat*
2	*iθnāni*	*iθnatāni*
3	*θalāθat*	*θalāθ*
4	*ʔarbaʕat*	*ʔarbaʕ*
5	*xamsat*	*xams*
6	*sittat*	*sitt*
7	*sabʕat*	*sabʕ*
8	*θamāniyat*	*θamānin*
9	*tisʕat*	*tisʕ*
10	*ʕašarat*	*ʕašr*

In the classical languages, the teens are usually expressed with a digit followed by the numeral 'ten', for example Arabic *ʔarbaʕat ʕašara* and Hebrew *ʔarbāʕā ʕaśar* '14 (M.)'. Note that in Hebrew and Arabic (among others) the form of 'ten' in the expression of teens exhibits the expected gender, in terms of its morphology, with the result that the digit and 'ten' appear to be of opposite gender. In Geʿez, the digit follows 'ten' in the expression of teens, and requires a conjunction, e.g., *ʕaśartu wa-ʔaħadu* '11 (M.)'; both units match in gender, unlike in Hebrew and Arabic. The order 'ten + digit' is common in Ethiopian Semitic, though not always with the conjunction, e.g., Amharic *asra säbatt* '17 (C.)'. In many of the modern languages, and in fact already in Akkadian, the digit and the numeral 'ten' have fused into a single word, for example Akkadian *erbēšeret* '14 (M.)', *xamiššeret* '15 (M.)', and Algerian Arabic *xməsṭaš* '15 (C.)'.

In some of the modern languages, gender distinction among the digits and teen numerals has been neutralized, resulting in a single form for both genders. This happens for both the digits and teens in most modern Ethiopian languages and in many NENA dialects, and with the teens in Arabic dialects.

We find two basic means of forming the tens in Semitic. In Akkadian and Ethiopian, the suffix *-ā* is attached to the numeral 'ten' to form twenty (e.g., Geʿez *ʕəśrā* '20') and to the digits 'three' to 'nine' to form 'thirty' through 'ninety' (e.g., Geʿez *xamsā* '50'). This suffix *-ā* is most likely the dual marker, at least historically. In Hebrew, Arabic, and Aramaic, the 'tens' are formed by adding a masculine plural suffix; 'ten' is used to form 'twenty', while the digits are used to form the remaining tens. So we find, for example, Hebrew *ʕeśrīm* '20' and *ʔarbāʕīm* '40'. It is likely that the dual suffix was originally used only for 'twenty' (the dual of 'ten') and the plural suffix for the others, and that the attested languages all exhibit levelling of the tens. That is to say, within each attested language, the words for 'twenty' through 'ninety' all contain the same suffixed morpheme, which is historically either the dual or masculine plural suffix.

3.4 VERBAL SYSTEM

As already mentioned above (§2.3), the most characteristic morphological feature of the Semitic languages is the use of consonantal roots in conjunction with vocalic templates. Nowhere is this more evident than in the verbal system. All Semitic verbs possess a lexical root, which is a set of consonants that contain the general lexical meaning. Each root can be used in conjunction with one or more verbal stems. Within each stem, vocalic templates, prefixes, and suffixes are used in order to construct each verbal form. In short, the roots carry the lexical meanings, while the templates and affixes carry the grammatical functions, indicating person, gender, number, tense, voice, and mood. This is illustrated by the following forms of the Biblical Hebrew root *KTB*, which has a basic meaning associated with writing: *yiktōb* 'he writes', *niktōb* 'we write', *kātab* 'he wrote', *kātabnū* 'we wrote', *kətōb* 'write! (M.SG.)', *kōtēb* 'is writing (M.SG.)', *niktab* 'he was written'.

The number of root consonants is normally three, and thus we can speak of the triliteral root. In the classical languages, we occasionally find quadriliteral roots (i.e., roots with four consonants); in some of the modern languages these are more frequent. Even verbs borrowed from non-Semitic languages are normally fitted into the root system, and so we find verbs like Modern Hebrew *fiksēs* 'he faxed' (root *FKSS*, from English 'fax') and Geʿez *mank^w^asa* 'he became a monk' (root *MNK^W^S*, from Greek *monakhos* 'monk'), both of which follow the normal patterns for quadriliteral roots. An interesting exception is Maltese, where borrowings are incorporated into the verbal system as words, rather than as roots, e.g., *iddownlowdja* 'he downloaded' (from English) and *irrakkomanda* 'he recommended' (from Italian *raccomandare*) (Hoberman and Aronoff 2003).

3.4.1 VERBAL STEMS

Every Semitic language has a basic, unmarked verbal stem. This is usually called the G-Stem in Semitic grammars, for German *Grundstamm* 'basic stem'. In addition to this basic stem, there are derived stems, which, among other things, are used to express causative, transitive, reflexive, reciprocal, passive, and iterative meanings. The stems are characterized either by prefixation or infixation of consonantal elements, or by phonological alteration of the root via gemination, vowel lengthening, or reduplication. Each of the major stem types will be treated in turn:

N-Stem: This stem is characterized by a prefix *n-*. In Akkadian, Hebrew, and Arabic, the N-Stem is usually passive or medio-passive, e.g., Hebrew *niptaḥ* 'be opened; open (intrans.)' vs. G-Stem *pātaḥ* 'open (trans.)'. In Aramaic, Ṣayhadic, and most Ethiopian languages, the N-Stem has been lost, while in Mehri and Geʿez, the N-Stem is only used with some quadriliteral roots. In Akkadian, quadriliteral verbs also appear most often in the N-Stem, and this is likely a Proto-Semitic feature (Gensler 1997); on a possible connection with Egyptian on this point, see Rubin (2004a). An attempt to trace the Afroasiatic origin of the N-Stem was made by Lieberman (1986).

D-Stem: This stem is characterized by gemination (D = doubling) of the second root consonant. The exact derivational function of this stem is difficult to pinpoint. Grammars of Semitic languages often describe the D-Stem as "intensive", though this vague label is not really warranted. It is true that some D-Stem verbs have a pluralic association (i.e., denoting activity on a plurality of objects), and this can sometimes make it seem as if the verbal action is intensified. For example, from the Arabic G-Stem *kasara* 'break (trans.)', we find the D-Stem *kassara* 'shatter (trans.) into many pieces'. But such verbs are relatively rare. More often, the D-Stem provides the factitive/causative for roots with stative meanings in the G-Stem (e.g., Mehri *mōlə?* 'fill' vs.

G-Stem *mīlə?* 'be full'), or is used to form denominative verbs (e.g., Mehri *ħōni* 'dye with henna', from *ħaynē?* 'henna'). In Ethiopian, the D-Stem has lost its derivational value and become simply lexical. A comprehensive study of the Akkadian D-Stem was made by Kouwenberg (1997); see also Joosten (1998).

C-Stem: The C-Stem normally adds a causative (= C) force to the root, e.g., NENA of Qaraqosh *?asmoxə* 'to cause to stand', G-Stem *smaxa* 'to stand'; Zay *?abälä* 'feed', G-Stem *bälä* 'eat'; Akkadian *šumk'utu* 'cause to fall', G-Stem *mak'ātu* 'fall'. In Akkadian, Ugaritic, and some of the Ṣayhadic language, this stem is characterized by a prefix *šV-* (< **sa-*), a morpheme which has a cognate in the Egyptian causative prefix *s-*. In the remainder of West Semitic, this prefix became *ha-* via a general sound change **s* > **h* (see above, §2.3), and was further weakened to *?a-* or *a-* in most languages. In Ethiopian, the C-Stem has become more productive, and we find not one C-Stem, but rather three C-Stems, which are built upon the G-, D-, and L-Stems, respectively.

T-Stem(s): T-Stems are characterized by a prefixed or infixed *t*, and are often found in conjunction with another verbal stem. For example, in Aramaic, we find a Gt-Stem, a Dt-Stem, and a Ct-Stem, that is, T-Stems made from the G-, D-, and C-Stems, respectively. The T-Stems have various functions in different languages, but, in general, they designate reflexives, reciprocals, passives, or medio-passives. In Aramaic and the Ethiopian languages, which have lost the N-Stem and internal passives (see below, §3.4.2), the T-Stems have become the primary means of expressing the passive. A lengthy study of the Semitic T-Stems was made by Diem (1982).

L-Stem: This is the only stem which is marked purely by vocalic means, namely by the lengthening (= L) of the vowel following the first root consonant. The L-Stem is found only in Arabic and the Ethiopian languages, though there are possible vestiges in Hebrew. In those ancient languages whose scripts do not indicate vowels (e.g., Ṣayhadic and Ugaritic), the L-Stem is impossible to detect. If it ever existed in Modern South Arabian, it has merged completely with the D-Stem. In Ethiopian, the L-Stem, like the D-Stem, has lost all derivational value and become simply lexical. Therefore, the only attested place the L-Stem has any special meaning is in Arabic, where it can have a variety of meanings, including associative action (e.g., *šāraka* 'enter into a partnership with', G-Stem *šarika* 'participate'), attempted action (e.g., *qātala* 'attempt to kill', G-Stem *qatala* 'kill'), and behavior (e.g., *ḥāsana* 'treat kindly', G-Stem *ḥasuna* 'be good'). These categories are not always applicable to modern Arabic dialects.

R-Stem(s): These stems are characterized by the reduplication (= R) of either the second or third root consonant. In Arabic, the two R-Stems, both of which are quite rare, involve reduplication (realized as gemination) of the third root consonant. Such verbs are most often connected with the acquisition of a color or physical trait or defect, e.g., *iswadda* 'become black' and *iḥwalla* 'squint; be cross-eyed'. This type of R-Stem has remnants in Hebrew, Modern South Arabian, and elsewhere, but it is productive (however rare) only in Arabic. In many modern Ethiopian languages, we find an R-Stem characterized by reduplication and gemination of the penultimate root consonant, and, among other things, it can have pluralic or repetitive associations. This stem is an internal development within the Ethiopian sub-family. Examples are Amharic *gänät'at't'älä* 'tear into pieces' (vs. *gänät't'älä* 'tear off, tear out'), *läwawwät'ä* 'vary (change often); change completely' (vs. *läwwät'ä* 'change') (Leslau 1995).

The number of verbal stems differs for each language. For example, in Syriac there are six stems (with vestiges of others), in Classical Arabic there are fifteen, and in NENA of Arbel there are just two. Moreover, the functions of a particular stem in one language do not always correspond with its functions in another language. For example, the Dt-Stem in Hebrew is often a reciprocal or reflexive (e.g., *hitnaššēq* 'kiss each other', D-Stem *niššēq* 'kiss'; *hitqaddēš* 'sanctify oneself', D-Stem *qiddēš* 'sanctify'), while in Syriac, it is simply a passive of the D-Stem (e.g., *ʔetqabbal* 'be received', D-Stem *qabbel* 'receive').

It is important to point out that a derived stem verb need not have a corresponding G-Stem verb. For example, in Arabic, the verb *ʔarsala* 'send' is a C-Stem verb, but the root RSL does not occur in the G-Stem. There is no other verb from which *ʔarsala* can be derived as a causative. As another example, in Mehri, the verb *šānōs* 'dare' (root *ʔNS*) is a Š1-Stem (a type of C-Stem specific to Modern South Arabian), but this is the only stem in which this root occurs. As these examples illustrate, it can happen that a derived stem verb is simply lexical and not "derived" at all. In Ethiopian, as noted above, the D- and L-Stems have become completely lexicalized. As a corollary to this, a verb that occurs in the G-Stem need not exhibit any derived stem. Also, except in those modern languages that have very few derived stems (e.g., NENA dialects), it is very rare that a verbal root can be used in all stems of a particular language.

3.4.2 VOICE

Semitic languages distinguish active and passive voice, though they differ with respect to how these categories are coded. There are two main morphological means of expressing passivity. The first way is by means of a derived verbal stem, usually a T-Stem or an N-Stem, as was already discussed above (§3.4.1). The second way is by means of what can be called an internal passive, meaning that the morphology is by means of the internal vowel pattern only. We find internal passives in Classical and Modern Standard Arabic (22), some modern Arabic dialects (Retsö 1983), to a limited extent in Hebrew (though rare in modern spoken Hebrew), in the older Aramaic dialects (all BCE), and to a limited extent in Modern South Arabian (23). For some epigraphic languages (e.g., Sabaic and Ugaritic) there is good syntactic evidence for internal passives, though the lack of written vowels in their respective scripts obscures the data.

Arabic

(22) *saʔal-nā,* *suʔil-nā*
ask:PAST.ACT-1PL, ask:PAST.PASS-1PL
'we asked, we were asked'

Omani Mehri

(23) *k'əbūr,* *k'əbēr*
bury:PAST.ACT.3M.SG, bury:PAST.PASS.3M.SG
'he buried, he was buried'

In addition to morphological passives, many languages also indicate passivity by syntactic means, either with an impersonal third person plural verb (24), or, less often, by means of an auxiliary verb and a past participle (25).

NENA (Qaraqosh)

(24) *bet-əḥ* *kəm-bane-lə* *šətqə*
house-3M.SG PAST-build:PRES.3PL-OBJ.3M.SG last.year
'His house was built last year.' (lit. 'His house, they built it last year.') (Khan 2002)

Maltese

(25) *ir-raġel* *kien* [or: *ġie*] *maqtul*
the-man be:PAST.3M.SG[come:PAST.3M.SG]kill:PART.PASS
'The man was killed.' (Ambros 1998)

In general, there is a strong tendency among the Semitic languages for the internal passive to be replaced by other means of indicating passivity, whether by derived verbal stems or by syntactic constructions.

3.4.3 VERBAL TENSE/ASPECT

The verbal system is the area in which the languages exhibit the greatest variation, and so an overview of the entire family is impossible in a brief format such as this. Here we will limit ourselves to some of the interesting developments in the realm of tense and aspect (Cohen 1984 and Kuryłowicz 1973 are important general works on this issue). For Proto-Semitic, suffice it to say that two basic verbal forms can be reconstructed, and it is likely that these mainly distinguished perfective and imperfective aspect. For some of the ancient languages, the issue of tense vs. aspect is a difficult one, and it is very difficult to say that the verbal system of, say, Akkadian or Biblical Hebrew, distinguished only tense or only aspect (see Joosten 2002 and Cook 2006 for recent discussion on this issue in Biblical Hebrew).

Past Tenses. In East Semitic (Akkadian), there existed a form known as the stative or verbal adjective, which was characterized by suffixed pronominal forms, as opposed to other verbal forms, which marked person and number by a set of prefixes (Huehnergard 1987b). This stative conjugation is found also in Egyptian, so it can be reconstructed for Afroasiatic. As already noted above (§1), in all of West Semitic, the inherited, prefixed past tense (e.g., Akkadian *nišrik'* 'we stole') was replaced by this suffixed conjugation (e.g., Arabic *saraqnā* 'we stole'). This is, therefore, a major development in the history of the Semitic verbal system. Subsequent to this, additional innovative past tenses developed in later forms of Aramaic and in Ethiopian. Already in the early first millennium CE, it became possible in some dialects of Aramaic—such as Syriac, Mandaic, and Jewish Babylonian Aramaic—to express a perfect tense by means of a construction which consisted of a past participle plus the preposition *l-* 'to, for' with a pronominal suffix (26).

Syriac
(26) *gbar lā ḥkīm l-ī*
man NEG know:PART.PASS.M.SG to-1SG
'I have not known a man.' (Nöldeke 1904)

Some believe that the preposition in this construction was originally instrumental in function, and so a phrase that meant something like 'it was known to/by me' was reinterpreted as 'I have known it'. However, since the preposition *l-* does not normally mark the agent of a passive, but does mark possession (see §4.8), others believe that a phrase like Syriac *ḥkīm lī* is a perfect tense, the literal equivalent of English 'I have known'. It has been suggested that such a development in Aramaic may have been a calque from Persian (Kutscher 1969; though see Bar-Asher 2007 for a counterargument). This new past tense, whatever its origin, has completely replaced the inherited past tense in most Neo-Aramaic languages.

In Ge'ez, there exists a verbal form variously known as the gerund, perfective active participle, converb, or verbal infinitive. This form is always subordinate to the main verb, and can be translated either by an English participial phrase or temporal clause (27).

Ge'ez

(27)	*wa-s'awim-o ...*	*rəxba*
	CONJ-fast:GER-3M.SG	be.hungry:PAST.3M.SG
	'Having fasted ... he was hungry' (Tropper 2002a)	

In Tigrinya, this equivalent form has become a simple past tense, replacing the inherited past tense in most contexts, e.g., *s'äwimu* (variant *s'oymu*) 'he fasted'. Similar developments have taken place in other modern Ethiopian languages.

In most other Semitic languages, secondary past tenses have developed, mostly by means of auxiliary verbs or other particles (Rubin 2005). For example, in many Arabic dialects, the past tense of the verb 'be' is used in combination with other verbal forms to create the past perfect (28), past progressive (29), and past habitual (30).

Iraqi (Muslim Baghdadi) Arabic

(28) *čān* *mākil* *min*
be:PAST.3M.SG eat:PART.M.SG when
xābar-t-a
telephone:PAST-1SG-3M.SG
'He had eaten when I telephoned him.'

(29) *čān* *da-yākul* *min*
be:PAST.3M.SG PROG-eat:NONPAST.3M.SG when
wuṣal-na
arrive:PAST-1PL
'He was eating when we arrived.'

(30) *čānat* *tirsim* *zēn*
be:PAST.3F.SG draw:NONPAST.3F.SG well
'She used to draw well.' (Erwin 1963)

Present Tenses. In Classical Arabic, Biblical Hebrew, Ge'ez, Akkadian, and other classical Semitic languages, there is a single non-past verbal tense that covers both present and future time. In many languages, however, new forms have developed that are specifically marked as general presents, present progressives, or present indicatives. In some languages, including later forms of Hebrew and Aramaic, the inherited participial form, which is nominal in origin, has become the present tense. In some other languages, a present tense is marked by a particle attached to an existing verbal form. Such particles derive most often from locative verbs or prepositions, i.e., the verbs 'be', 'sit', 'stand', or 'lie', or the preposition 'in, at' (Rubin 2005). For example, the prefix *da-* in Iraqi Arabic (*qa-* in Jewish and Christian dialects) is attached to the inherited non-past form, and indicates a present progressive, continuous, or habitual (31; cf. also 29, above). This prefix derives from *qāʕid*, a participial form of the verb 'sit'.

Christian Baghdadi Arabic
(31) *qa-ṭəṭbəx* *ṭabīx*
PROG-cook:NONPAST.3F.SG stew
'She is cooking a stew.' (Abu-Haidar 1991)

In some NENA dialects, including the Jewish dialect of Sulemaniyya, a present indicative is marked by a prefix *k-*. This derives from an earlier prefix *qā-*, used in older dialects of Aramaic to mark a continuous or habitual present, which ultimately derives from a form *qāʔem*, a participial form of the verb 'stand'.

In most Ethiopian languages, the inherited non-past form can be combined with a form of the verb 'be'. This compound form indicates the non-past in a main clause, while the inherited, simple non-past is used in subordinate or negative clauses. Thus in many Ethiopian languages, including Amharic, the present and future are not normally distinguished.

Future Tenses. Explicit future tenses have developed in a number of Semitic languages. Often markers of the future derive from grammaticalized forms of verbs meaning 'go' or 'want', though other sources are well attested (Rubin 2005). For example, in Egyptian Arabic (and several other Arabic dialects), the future-marking prefix *ħa-* is derived from the participle *rāyiħ* 'going' (32). Several dialects of NENA have a future-marking particle *bəd-* (variants *bət-*, *b-*, *d-*), which is derived from an earlier Aramaic construction *bāʕe d-* 'want that' or *bʕe d-* 'it is desired that' (33).

Egyptian Arabic

(32) *ħa-yirgaʕ* *bukṛa*
FUT-return:NONPAST.3M.SG tomorrow
'He will return tomorrow.' (Abdel-Massih et al. 1979)

NENA (Barwar)

(33) *qaṭuθ-i bəd-mnagra-lux*
cat-1SG FUT-gnaw:PRES.3F.SG-OBJ.2M.SG
'My cat will gnaw you.' (Khan 2008a)

In Mehri (and the closely related dialects of Ḥarsusi and Baṭḥari), the active participle has come to indicate future tense, with the result that the inherited non-past form has become the basic present tense.

3.4.4 MOOD

All Semitic languages possess an imperative form (34), though in nearly all of the languages, imperatives occur only in positive commands. Negative commands are normally expressed by negating another verbal form, normally the non-past (35) or the jussive (on this term, see below). Negation of the actual imperative form is found only in some Neo-Aramaic dialects, e.g., in the Jewish NENA dialect of Arbel (36), but not in the Christian NENA dialect of Qaraqosh.

Old Babylonian Akkadian

(34) *šupur*
send:IMPER.M.SG
'Send!'

(35) *lā tašappar*
NEG send:NONPAST.2M.SG
'Don't send!' (Huehnergard 2005b)

NENA (Arbel)

(36) *la si*
NEG go:IMPER.SG
'Don't go!' (Khan 1999)

There are no first or third person imperatives in Semitic, though there is a jussive mood that fulfills the function of the imperative for these persons. The jussive in Proto-Semitic seems to have been identical in shape to the perfective verbal form. In Akkadian, the jussive (normally termed the "precative" in grammars of Akkadian) is distinguished from the inherited perfective by the addition of an asseverative (or topicalizing) particle *l(V)-* (Huehnergard 1983; Testen 1993); cf. Akkadian *illik* 'he went' and *l-illik* 'let him go, may he go'. In West Semitic, the inherited perfective (of the shape **prefix + CCVC*) lost its function as the normal indicator of past tense (see above, §1, §3.4.3), but the form itself survived in its jussive function. This is most evident in Modern South Arabian and in Ethiopian Semitic; cf. Geʿez *nabara* 'he sat' and jussive *yənbar* 'let him sit, may he sit'.

The situation in the rest of West Semitic, i.e., Central Semitic, is slightly more complex. The inherited perfective form, in combination with a suffix **-u* (originally a marker of subordination) came to indicate non-past, replacing the inherited non-past form (Rubin 2005). The result is that in Central Semitic there was a form of the shape **prefix + CCVC* that indicated the jussive, and a form **prefix + CCVC-u* that indicated non-past. This situation is found in Classical and Modern Standard Arabic. As in Akkadian, the Arabic jussive (when used as a true jussive, i.e., as a first or third person imperative) is preceded by an asseverative particle, e.g., indicative non-past *yašrab-u* 'he drinks' vs. jussive *li-yašrab* 'let him drink, may he drink'. In some Central Semitic languages, including modern Arabic dialects, Hebrew, and Aramaic, the final short *-u* of this innovative non-past form was lost, with the result that the non-past and jussive merged in most environments. So, in Biblical Hebrew, for example, the jussive is most often not morphologically distinct from the non-past, and a jussive meaning must be gleaned from context. Compare examples (37) and (38), both of which contain the identical verbal form *yišpōṭ*.

Biblical Hebrew

(37) *hū yišpōṭ* *tēbēl bə-ṣedeq*
he judge:NONPAST.3M.SG world with-righteousness
'He judges the world with righteousness.' (Psalm 9:9)

(38) *yišpōṭ* YHWH *bēn-ī*
judge:JUSS.3M.SG DN between-1SG
u-bēn-ekā
and-between-2M.SG
'May the LORD judge between me and you.' (Gen. 16:5)

In addition to the indicative and jussive moods, Arabic possesses a subjunctive mood, formed with the same verbal base plus a suffix *-a* (e.g., *yašrab-a*). The subjunctive is used in subordinate clauses, most often following subordinating conjunctions. In Akkadian, subordination is marked by attaching the suffix *-u* to verbs (20, in §3.2.3); this is the same suffix that in Central Semitic marks the indicative.

The jussive and subjunctive moods of the written language are absent from the modern Arabic dialects, due, as already noted, to the loss of final short vowels. However, there is some distinction of mood by innovative means. In some of the dialects in which a present tense marker has developed, lack of this marker can indicate a subjunctive or jussive. In example (39), we see the Syrian Arabic present tense marker *b-* used in an indicative phrase. In example (40), on the other hand, we see how the absence of this (or any other) pre-verbal marker can indicate a jussive meaning.

Syrian Arabic
(39) *b-ināmu* *ʕal-ʔəṣṭūḥ* *bə-l-lēl*
PRES-sleep:NONPAST.3M.PL on.the-roof in-the-night
'They sleep on the roof at night.'

(40) *yəxrab* *bēt-o*
be.ruined:NONPAST.3M.SG house-3M.SG
'May his house be ruined!' (Cowell 1964)

The situation in many Neo-Aramaic dialects parallels that of Syrian Arabic, which is to say that a subjunctive or jussive can be marked by the absence of an overt present or future tense prefix.

Akkadian exhibits another verbal form, known as the "ventive", that is sometimes called a mood by Semitists (e.g., Moscati

1964), presumably with the idea that "mood" covers any type of verbal modification. The ventive is really a type of verbal deixis, with no modal functions. In Old Babylonian Akkadian, the ventive suffix has the allomorphs *-(a)m* and *-nim*, and may be attached to any finite verbal form. It gives the sense of direction or activity towards the speaker: contrast *illik* 'went' and ventive *illik-am* 'he came'; *ublū* 'they brought (there)' and ventive *ublū-nim* 'they brought here'; and *ūṣi* 'I went out' and ventive *ūṣi-am* 'I came out here' (von Soden 1995). Not coincidentally, the first common singular dative pronominal object suffix also has the allomorphs *-(a)m* and *-nim* in Akkadian, e.g., *taddin-am* 'you gave to me'. It is unclear if the Akkadian ventive has parallels in West Semitic. It has been argued, rather convincingly, that the suffix *-ā* that can be attached to Biblical Hebrew imperatives has a ventive function (Fassberg 1999). On other connections between the Akkadian ventive and West Semitic morphemes, see the recent study of Hasselbach (2006).

3.4.5 PHRASAL VERBS

Phrasal verbs (also known as composite verbs) are a characteristic feature of the modern Ethiopian Semitic languages. In these constructions, which have developed under Cushitic influence, a verbal concept is expressed by a fixed element and a conjugated form of the verb 'say' or, much less often (and not in all the languages), 'make', 'name', or 'become'. Examples are Amharic *k'uč'č' alä* 'he sat down', *däss aläw* 'he was happy' (lit. 'it was pleasing to him'), and *zəmm alä* 'he was quiet', all based on *alä* 'he said' (Leslau 1995); Wolane *ʔənt'əšš balä* 'he sneezed', *lodd balä* 'he was slow', and *guff balä* 'it smoked (intrans.)', all based on *balä* 'he said' (Meyer 2006); and Tigré *kaf belä* 'he sat', *koy belä* 'he hurried', and *ləhəb belä* 'he sweated', all based on *belä* 'he said' (Raz 1983). Only the verb is conjugated, as in Tigré *koy ʔəbe* 'I hurried', *koy nəbe* 'we hurried', *koy beläw* 'they hurried', *koy ləblo* 'they hurry', and *koy bal* 'hurry!'. Many of the fixed elements that are part of these phrasal verbs do not occur independently, and so it is often not possible to give the fixed elements an independent meaning.

A parallel to the Ethiopian phrasal verbs can be found in some Neo-Aramaic dialects. In the Jewish NENA dialect of Sulemaniyya, for example, we find phrasal verbs that have a verbal element (most often 'do', 'become', 'give', 'come', or 'bring') and a fixed element (Khan 2004). The fixed element is normally a loanword, and the phrasal verb itself is in most cases a calque from Kurdish. Examples are *ʕaraqa wala* 'sweat' and *rani wala* 'hunt' (from *wala* 'to do'); *tiffe dyaya* 'spit' and *skita dyaya* 'stab' (from *dyaya* 'to give', itself a Kurdish loan); and *mirxew yaʔa* 'snore' and *jigrew yaʔa* 'hate, be angry' (from *yaʔa* 'to come'). In Neo-Mandaic, we find similar phrasal verbs, which are usually calques from Persian (Häberl 2009).

3.5 ADVERBS

Semitic languages normally have a limited set of words that function only as adverbs. Each language has numerous demonstrative adverbs (e.g., Yemeni Arabic *hāna* 'here', *hānāk* 'there'), adverbs of manner (e.g., Syriac *hākanā* 'thus'), and adverbs of time (e.g., Hebrew *ʔetmōl* 'yesterday'). However, most languages do not have a productive means of deriving adverbs, and so adverbial expression is often done by means of a prepositional phrase (41), or even an unmarked adjective (42). Alternatively, in a number of the languages, an adverbial sense can be expressed through verb serialization, sometimes termed "hendiadys" in Semitic grammars (43).

Modern Hebrew

(41) *bə-simxa,* *b-ofen* *tivʕi,* *bli* *kavana*
with-happiness, with-manner natural, without intention
'happily, naturally, unintentionally'

(42) *hi* *mədaberet* *barur*
she speak:PRES.F.SG clear[ADJ].M.SG
'She speaks clearly.' (Coffin and Bolozky 2005)

Geʿez

(43) *k'adam-ku* *bas'āḥ-ku*
precede:PAST-1SG arrive:PAST-1SG
'I arrived early.' (Tropper 2002a)

Ethiopian Semitic languages, like Amharic, are particularly fond of using verbal phrases to express adverbial connotations (Leslau 1995).

In Akkadian, we do find an identifiable adverbial marker, namely the suffix *-iš*, which, as already mentioned above (§3.2.2), can be used to form adverbs from adjectives, for example, *damk'iš* 'well', from *damik'-* 'good'.

In Syriac and Christian Palestinian Aramaic, we also find a productive adverbial morpheme. The suffix *-āʔīt* forms adverbs of quality and manner from adjectives and some nouns. Examples are Syriac *šappīrāʔīt* 'beautifully' (cf. *šappīr* 'beautiful'), *ʔalāhāʔīt* 'divinely' (cf. *ʔalāh* 'God', *ʔalāhāy* 'divine'), and *sūryāʔīt* 'in Syriac' (cf. *sūryā* 'Syria'). This suffix is known also from Classical Mandaic and Jewish Babylonian Aramaic, though it is not common in either dialect. On the derivation of this Aramaic adverbial suffix, see Gensler (2000) and Butts (2010), the former of which also has some discussion of the Akkadian adverbial *-iš*.

4 Syntax

4.1 Word Order

Proto-Semitic seems to have been a VSO language, that is, the standard word order was Verb–Subject–Object. This is the usual word order for a number of the ancient languages, including Biblical Hebrew, Arabic (44), and Ge‘ez. In addition, modifiers such as adjectives (45), genitives (46), and relative clauses (47) followed their head noun.

Classical Arabic

(44) *xarajati* *l-marʔat-u* *mina* *l-bayt-i*
go.out:PAST.3F.SG the-woman-NOM from the-house-GEN
'The woman went out from the house.'

(45) *ʔal-bayt-u* *l-bārid-u*
the-house-NOM the-cold-NOM
'the cold house'

Biblical Hebrew

(46) *derek* *ham-melek*
highway[CONSTR] the-king
'the king's highway' (Num. 20:17)

Ge‘ez

(47) *bəʔsi* *za-mota*
man.NOM REL-die:PAST.3M.SG
'the man who died'

A number of the languages, both ancient and modern, deviate from the standard Semitic type. Akkadian adopted SOV word order as a result of contact with Sumerian, though all modifiers still normally follow their head noun (Deutscher 2000). Modern Hebrew, Neo-Aramaic languages, and a number of modern Arabic dialects (e.g., Iraqi, Chadian) exhibit SVO word order (on Arabic, see Brustad 2000). In Modern Hebrew, this is the result of general European influence. In these languages, as in Akkadian, modifiers still follow their head noun.

The most drastic changes in word ordering are found in the modern Ethiopian languages. All modern Ethiopian Semitic languages exhibit SOV word order (48), as a result of Cushitic influence (Leslau 1945a). In addition, nearly all, if not all, the languages place adjectives, genitives (49), and relatives (50) before their head nouns.

Zay

(48) *äya t-etate* *tä-set* *mät'āhu*
I with-that:F.SG with-woman come:PAST.1SG
'I came with that woman.'

(49) *yä-šum-i* *gār*
of-chief-the house
'the chief's house'

(50) *gəɲi-y* *yä-gaɲ-e* *bäyu*
dog-ACC REL-find:PAST.3M.SG-the child
'the child who found the dog' (Leslau 1999)

4.2 POSITIONAL RELATIONS

All Semitic languages have prepositions, though some languages also have postpositions and circumpositions. Prepositions are the norm in most Semitic languages, including all of the ancient languages. In languages that have retained case marking, prepositions always govern the genitive case. Semitic prepositions are of two types. There are those that are cliticized to their head noun (51) and those that are treated as independent words (52). The former type usually number only three to four in a given language, with the great majority of prepositions treated as separate units.

Classical Arabic
(51) *bi-l-bayt-i*
in-the-house-GEN
'in the house'

(52) *mina l-bayt-i*
from the-house-GEN
'from the house'

In nearly all of the languages, the expression of the pronominal object of a preposition is by means of a pronominal suffix attached to the preposition (see §3.1.2). For example, following are the forms of the Omani Mehri preposition *h-* 'to, for' ('to me, to you', etc.).

<table>
<tr><th></th><th>SG</th><th>DU</th><th>PL</th></tr>
<tr><td>1st C</td><td>háyni</td><td rowspan="3">háki</td><td>hīn</td></tr>
<tr><td>2nd M</td><td>hūk</td><td>hīkəm</td></tr>
<tr><td>2nd F</td><td>hayš</td><td>hīkən</td></tr>
<tr><td>3rd M</td><td>həh</td><td rowspan="2">háhi</td><td>hīhəm</td></tr>
<tr><td>3rd F</td><td>hīs</td><td>hīsən</td></tr>
</table>

Some modern Ethiopian languages, on the other hand, use the independent forms of the pronouns with prepositions (as well as with postpositions and circumpositions); cf. Amharic *wädäne* 'to me' (< *wädä* 'to' + *əne* 'I') and *kässu* 'from him' (< *kä* 'from' + *əssu* 'he').

In modern Ethiopian Semitic languages, there is a greater tendency towards circumpositions and postpositions. The postpositions are often the result of grammaticalized nouns, for which there was a preceding genitive phrase used as a modifier (53–54). The prepositional elements of the circumpositions in Amharic can be omitted in both speech and writing, resulting in a postposition (Leslau 1995).

Amharic
(53) *bä-bet wəsṭ* (< **bä-yä-bet wəsṭ*)
PREP-house in (< in-of-house interior)
'in the house' (< 'in the interior of the house')

(54) *b-antä bet* (< **bä-yä-antä bet*)
PREP-you according.to (< in-of-you house)
'according to you' (< 'in the house of you')

In some South Ethiopian languages, if a noun is preceded by a modifier, a preposition is repeated for each element (48, in §4.1). This was also the case in Soqoṭri a hundred years ago (55). However, in modern Soqoṭri, only the second occurrence of the preposition has survived, with the result that prepositions can be embedded within a noun phrase (56) (Lonnet 1998).

Soqoṭri (circa 1900)
(55) *min di-heh min əmboriye*
from of-he from children
'from his children'

Soqoṭri (circa 1990)
(56) *di-hoh k-əmboriye*
of-I with-children
'with my children'

4.3 AGREEMENT

There are a number of issues pertaining to agreement in Semitic that are noteworthy. The case of the numerals, which seem to exhibit reverse gender concord, was already discussed above (§3.3). It was also already noted above (§3.2.1) that in languages in which the dual has ceased to become a productive category (e.g., Hebrew), fossilized dual forms are treated as plural for agreement purposes.

Attributive adjectives in Semitic normally agree with their head nouns in gender, number, and case (where applicable, and referring to the inherited Proto-Semitic case markers only); in Central Semitic (with the exception of Neo-Aramaic) and in Mehri, attributive adjectives also agree in definiteness (57). A noun with a possessive suffix is considered definite for the purposes of agreement (58). As a general tendency, agreement rules are less strict in Ethiopian Semitic.

Classical Arabic

(57) *ʔal-marʔat-u* *l-ḥasan-at-u*
the-woman-NOM the-beautiful-F.SG-NOM
'the beautiful woman'

Biblical Hebrew

(58) *bēt-əkā* *hag-gādōl*
house-2M.SG the-big
'your big house'

In many Semitic languages, a distinction is made in the agreement of attributive and predicative adjectives. For those languages in which attributive adjectives agree in definiteness (i.e., Central Semitic languages [except Neo-Aramaic] and Mehri), predicative adjectives do not do so. Compare the following examples (59–60) with the two phrases above (57–58).

Classical Arabic

(59) *ʔal-marʔat-u* *ḥasan-at-un*
the-woman-NOM beautiful-F.SG-NOM.INDEF
'The woman is beautiful.'

Biblical Hebrew

(60) *bēt-əkā* *gādōl*
house-2M.SG big
'Your house is big.'

In Akkadian, predicative adjectives are marked with a special set of gender and number markers. Moreover, there is a special set of enclitic personal pronouns that are attached to the adjective—which itself has no case, gender, or number markers—to indicate predication (61). Because suffixes have developed for all persons, this construction is often referred to as a stative "tense". Though this construction is not verbal in origin, it is often convenient to think of it as verbal in Akkadian. This is because the predicative adjectives have verbal properties, in that they are associated with verbal roots; indicate person, number and gender; can take the marker of subordination; and can take a ventive morpheme. Indeed, in West Semitic, this developed into a true past tense (as noted in §1).

Old Babylonian Akkadian

(61) *awīl-um marus'-Ø, awīlt-um mars'-at, mars'-āku*
man-NOM sick-3M.SG, woman-NOM sick-3F.SG, sick-1SG
'the man is sick, the woman is sick, I am sick'
(Huehnergard 2005b)

Agreement in Classical and Modern Standard Arabic is slightly more complex than in the other languages. The above rules given for attributive and predicative adjectives apply when the noun is singular or dual. When the noun is plural (and occasionally also when it is a dual), agreement is dependent on animacy. For nouns referring to humans, agreement follows that of singular nouns, so masculine plural nouns referring to humans take masculine plural adjectives and feminine plural nouns take feminine plural adjectives (62). For all other nouns, plurals are treated as feminine singular (63).

Modern Standard Arabic

(62) *ʔaz-zuwwār-u r-rasmiyy-ūna*
the-visitors[M.PL]-NOM the-official-M.PL.NOM
'the official visitors'

(63) *taqālīd-un masīḥiyy-at-un*
traditions[M.PL]-NOM.INDEF Christian-F.SG-NOM.INDEF
'Christian traditions' (Ryding 2005)

Agreement between nouns and verbs in Classical and Modern Standard Arabic exhibits similar idiosyncrasies. When a verb precedes its subject (as is normally the case), its form is always singular, even when the subject is dual or plural. The gender of the verb is determined by whether or not the subject refers to humans. Masculine dual or plural subjects referring to humans are preceded by a masculine singular verb (64), while non-human masculine dual or plural subjects (usually) and all feminine subjects are preceded by feminine singular verbs (65). For singular nouns, gender concord between nouns and verbs is strict.

Modern Standard Arabic

(64) *ḍaħik-a* *ṭ-ṭullab-u*
laugh:PAST-3M.SG the-students[M.PL]-NOM
'The students laughed.' (Ryding 2005)

(65) *ʔittafaq-ati* *l-wufūd-u*
agree:PAST-3F.SG the-delegations[M.PL]-NOM
'The delegations agreed.' (Mace 1998)

4.4 COMPARISON

In the Semitic languages, we find both analytical (syntactic) and inflectional (morphological) means of comparison, though the former is more common. In Arabic, which has an inflectional comparative, the comparative form of the adjective has the basic pattern *ʔaCCaC*, as in *ṭawīl* 'long, tall', *ʔaṭwal* 'longer, taller'; *ħasan* 'beautiful', *ʔaħsan* 'more beautiful'. The comparative form (normally called in Arabic grammars the "elative" form) can also denote an intensive, i.e., 'very tall', 'very beautiful', as required by context. When it occurs with the definite article (66) or as the first member of a genitive chain (67), the comparative form indicates a superlative.

Classical Arabic

(66) *ʔar-rajul-u* *l-ʔaṭwal-u*
the-man-NOM the-tall:COMPAR-NOM
'the tallest man'

(67) *ʔaṭwal-u* *r-rijāli*
tall:COMPAR-NOM[CONSTR] the-men-GEN
'the tallest of the men'

A very few adjectives of the pattern **ʔaCCaC* are found lexicalized in Biblical Hebrew (e.g., *ʔakzār* 'cruel'), but it is unclear if these are archaisms or borrowings. Comparison in Hebrew, like most other Semitic languages, is purely analytical. That is, there is no morphological form indicating comparison (68).

Biblical Hebrew

(68) *ʕam* *gādōl* *wā-rām* *mimmen-nū*
people great and-tall from-1PL
'a people greater and taller than us' (Deut. 1:28)

The Arabic comparative pattern *ʔaCCaC* is likely related to the Akkadian pattern *šuCCuC*, which can give the sense of 'very' or 'most' to adjectives, e.g., *šurbû* 'very great' from *rabû* 'great' (Speiser 1952). The extension of this type of intensive pattern into a true inflectional comparative is likely an internal development within Arabic. Some languages—Neo-West Aramaic and Mehri, for example—have borrowed the inflectional comparative pattern *ʔaCCaC* from Arabic (though in Mehri it is rather rare).

4.5 COORDINATION

Coordination of elements or phrases is normally indicated by means of a proclitic or enclitic particle. The most common of these is the prefixed particle **wa-* (in some languages realized as *wə-* or *u-*), which is found in nearly all Semitic languages, with the notable exception of some modern Ethiopian languages (69). In a few South Ethiopian languages, *-wa* has become suffixed (70).

Chadian Arabic
(69) *al-gitt wa-l-jidād*
the-cat and-the-chickens
'the cat and the chickens' (Jullien de Pommerol 1999)

Zay
(70) *bok'olu-wa färäz lām būrä*
mule-and horse cow ox
'a mule, a horse, a cow, and an ox' (Leslau 1999)

The enclitic coordinating particle **-ma* is known from Akkadian and many Ethiopian languages (71). In some Central Semitic languages, most notably in Ugaritic (Tropper 2000a), this particle seems to be a sort of topicalizer, as it also often can be in Akkadian.

Amharic
(71) *č'äw bärbärre-mm*
salt pepper-and
'salt and pepper' (Leslau 1995)

In Akkadian, the coordinators *u* (< **wa-*) and *-ma* have slightly different functions. For example, two clauses coordinated with *u* can be reversed without altering any meaning; not so for clauses coordinated with *-ma* (Huehnergard 2005b). Slightly different semantic distinctions are made in Ethiopian languages that have both of these particles (e.g., Zay; see Meyer 2005).

The proclitic coordinating particle **pa-*, indicating sequential coordination ('and then'), is found in some Central Semitic languages, namely Ugaritic, Arabic, Ṣayhadic, Sam'alian, and a few Aramaic dialects. In a number of Ethiopian languages, we find an enclitic coordinator with an enclitic element *n*, including Amharic *-nnā* and Tigrinya *-n*.

Although every Semitic language possesses at least one coordinating conjunction, asyndetic coordination is also well attested in the family (72–73).

Tigrinya
(72) *rəʔəy-ä* *sämiʕ-e*
see:PAST-1SG hear:PAST-1SG
'I saw and I heard' (Leslau 1941)

Egyptian (Imperial) Aramaic (unvocalized)
(73) *ʔzl-t* *hškħ-t* *l-ʔħyqr*
go:PAST.1SG find:PAST.1SG ACC-Ahiqar
'I went and found Ahiqar' (Muraoka and Porten 2003)

4.6 Copular Clauses

In the classical Semitic languages, and in many modern Semitic languages, there is no expressed copula, at least not in the present tense (74–75). This situation can be presumed for Proto-Semitic.

Biblical Hebrew
(74) *mī* *ʔattā*
who you:M.SG
'Who are you?' (Gen. 27:18)

Omani Mehri
(75) *ðōməh ħayr-i u tēθ tēθ-i*
this:M.SG donkey-1SG and woman woman-1SG
'This is my donkey, and the woman is my wife.'
(Rubin 2010b)

Most languages make use of a verb 'to be' in the past and future tenses, but the individual verbs vary (i.e., the roots used) (76–77).

Biblical Hebrew
(76) *ʕebed hāyītā bə-ʔereṣ miṣrayim*
slave be:PAST.2M.SG in-land[CONSTR] Egypt
'You were a slave in the land of Egypt.' (Deut. 15:15)

Omani Mehri
(77) *hēt wək'ōna a-mlək-həm*
you:SG be:FUT.M.SG the-king-3M.PL
'You will be their king.' (Rubin 2010b)

In many of the languages that normally do not express a copula in the present tense, a demonstrative or personal pronoun can fill the spot of a copula, in order to make clear that a separate subject and predicate are being expressed (78–79).

Geʻez
(78) *zəntu wəʔətu nəguś*
this:M.SG he king
'This is the king.'

Modern Hebrew
(79) *našim hen mi-noga u-gvarim hem mi-madim*
women they:F from-Venus and-men they:M from-Mars
'Women are from Venus and men are from Mars.'
(Coffin and Bolozky 2005)

A number of modern languages, including modern Ethiopian languages, Neo-Aramaic languages, and some Arabic dialects, have developed present-tense copulas, most often from grammaticalized demonstratives or presentative particles (Rubin 2005).

4.7 EXISTENTIAL CLAUSES

Many Semitic languages have developed existential particles, the sources of which are varied (Rubin 2005). Some of these particles derive from locative prepositions. For example, a number of Arabic dialects (e.g., Syrian, Egyptian, Chadian) use *fī* 'there is/are' (<*fī-hi* 'in it'), and Geʿez uses *bo* 'there is/are' (lit. 'in it'). A few languages have particles that are fossilized forms of the verb 'to be', including Moroccan Arabic *kāyn* and, most likely, Iraqi Arabic *ʔaku* (both derived from forms of the Arabic verb *kāna* 'to be'). The origin of the existential particles in the Northwest Semitic languages—Hebrew *yēš*, Aramaic *ʔīt*, Ugaritic *ʔiθ*, etc.—is not totally clear, though they are almost certainly related to the Akkadian verb *išûm* 'have'. It is quite plausible that 'have' is the original meaning of this root, and that the existential meaning is secondary; cf. the French construction *il y a*. In some languages, there is a special negative existential particle, for example, Biblical Hebrew *ʔēn* 'there is/are not' (vs. *yēš* 'there is/are').

Even languages that have a special existential particle often make use of the simple verb 'to be' to express existence in the past and future (80–81).

Biblical Hebrew

(80)	*rimmā*	*lō*	*hāyətā*	*b-ō*
	maggot.COLL	NEG	be:PAST.3F.SG	in-3M.SG

'There were no maggots in it.' (Exod. 16:24)

(81)	*lō*	*yihye*	*māṭār*
	NEG	be:FUT.3M.SG	rain

'There will be no rain.' (Deut. 11:17)

A few Arabic dialects form existential constructions with the adverb 'there', just as in English (82).

Maltese

(82)	*hemm*	*ilpup*	*f'Malta*
	there	wolves	in-Malta

'Are there wolves in Malta?' (Ambros 1998)

Sometimes, as in Mehri, an existential is simply understood, and no verb, adverb, or particle is used (83; see also 93, in §4.9)

Omani Mehri

(83) *xəṭərāt ḥōkəm b-ərḥəbēt*
once ruler in-town
'once there was a ruler in a town' (Rubin 2010b)

4.8 POSSESSION

It has already been noted above (§3.1.1, §3.1.2) that pronominal possession in Proto-Semitic was indicated by means of a pronominal suffix, and that some languages have developed an independent possessive adjective. It was also noted that a genitive relationship between two nouns was indicated by means of a construct phrase (genitive chain), but that some languages have developed an independent genitive exponent. It is unclear whether Proto-Semitic had a verb corresponding to English 'have'. Akkadian has the verb *išûm* 'have', which is cognate with an existential particle in West Semitic (e.g., Hebrew *yēš*, Ugaritic *ʔiθ*). As mentioned above (§4.7), we cannot know for sure whether an original existential developed into a verb of possession in Akkadian, or whether a verb of possession developed into an existential in some West Semitic languages, since both scenarios are easily conceivable. Regardless, the West Semitic languages make use of various phrasal constructions to express the equivalent of 'have'. These constructions normally contain a locative (84), comitative (85), or dative preposition; the last of these is sometimes found in conjunction with an existential particle (86) or a verb of existence. In Ethiopian languages, we find a construction consisting of an existential particle or a verb of existence plus a suffixed object pronoun (87).

Maltese

(84) *omm-i għand-ha qattus*
mother-1SG at-3F.SG cat
'My mother has a cat.' (Ambros 1998)

Omani Mehri

(85)	*ḥām-əy*	*š-īs*	*amōl*	*mēkən*
	mother-1SG	with-3F.SG	property	much

‘My mother had a lot of property.’ (Rubin 2010b)

Biblical Hebrew

(86)	*yēš*	*l-ī*	*tiqwā*
	EXIST	to-1SG	hope

‘I have hope.’ (Ruth 1:12)

Wolane

(87)	*mekine*	*ʔale-ɲɲ*
	car	exist:NONPAST.3M.SG-OBJ.1SG

‘I have a car.’ (Meyer 2006)

4.9 INTERROGATIVES

All Semitic languages exhibit interrogative pronouns and adverbs, which are, on the whole, typologically unremarkable. Occasionally, interrogatives show some syntactic peculiarities. For example, in Egyptian Arabic, interrogatives normally occupy the position in the sentence occupied by the questioned constituent. The result is that interrogatives in Egyptian Arabic—usually standing for direct objects, indirect objects, or adverbial clauses—are often phrase-final (88–89). In most other Arabic dialects, as in other Semitic languages, interrogatives are normally fronted (90).

Egyptian Arabic

(88)	*ʔaṛē-t*	*il-kitāb*	*lē*
	read:PAST-2M.SG	the-book	why

‘Why did you read the book?’ (Abdel-Massih et al. 1979)

(89)	*ʕāwiz*	*ē*
	want:PRES.M.SG	what

‘What do you want?’ (Woidich 2006)

Syrian Arabic

(90)	*lēš*	*ṭləʕ-t*
	why	go.out:PAST-2M.SG

‘Why did you go out?’ (Cowell 1964)

A number of languages also possess a special interrogative particle, used to turn a statement into a question. Often such particles are proclitic or enclitic elements. Examples are Classical and Modern Standard Arabic *ʔa-*, Biblical Hebrew *hă-*, Geʿez *-nu* and *-hu* (91), Tigrinya *-do* (92), and Amharic *-nə*. The Arabic, Hebrew, and Geʿez particles are all attached to the first constituent in the sentence, while the Tigrinya and Amharic particles are sentence-final. Examples of non-clitic interrogative particles are Classical and Modern Standard Arabic *hal*, Hebrew (mainly post-Biblical) *haʔim*, and Mehri *wəlɛ̄* (93). Most of these particles, whether clitic or non-clitic, are optional. Some are restricted to certain types of questions (e.g., yes-or-no questions).

Geʿez
(91) *zanta-nu* *gabar-ki*
this:ACC-INTERROG do:PAST.2F.SG
'Did you do this?' (Dillmann 1907)

Tigrinya
(92) *lomi* *təmhərti* *ʔāllo-do*
today school EXIST-INTERROG
'Is there school today?' (Melles 2001)

Omani Mehri
(93) *wəlɛ̄* *śī* *ʔāyd*
INTERROG any sardine.COLL
'Are there any sardines?' (Rubin 2010b)

4.10 RELATIVE CLAUSES

In Proto-Semitic, relative clauses could be asyndetic, in which case the antecedent was in the construct state, or syndetic, in which case the antecedent was followed by a determinative-relative pronoun that declined for gender, number, and case. The former type is found in Akkadian (20, in §3.2.3) and in Ṣayhadic, with vestiges in Geʿez, Hebrew, and elsewhere. The latter type is widespread in Semitic, though the inherited relative has in many languages become indeclinable (i.e., a single frozen form survives). For example, while a fully declinable relative pronoun existed in Old Akkadian (and Eblaite), in Old Babylonian Akkadian, the masculine singular accusative form *ša* became an indeclinable relative pronoun; in Aramaic, the masculine singular genitive form *dī* (later *d-*) underwent the same development (94).

Biblical Aramaic

(94)	*ḥelm-ā*	*dī*	*ḥăzēt*
	dream-the	REL	see:PAST.1SG

'the dream that I saw' (Daniel 2:26)

In the Canaanite dialects—most importantly, Hebrew and Phoenician—a noun **ʔaθar* 'place' has been grammaticalized as a relative pronoun (95), replacing the inherited forms, though the Proto-Semitic relative is attested as such in some archaic Biblical Hebrew passages and in archaic Byblian Phoenician. Huehnergard (2006a) presents a very detailed discussion of this development.

Biblical Hebrew

(95)	*ʔēlle*	*had-dəbārīm*	*ʔăšer*	*dibber*	*mōše*
	these	the-words	REL	speak:PAST.3M.SG	Moses

'These are the words that Moses spoke.' (Deut. 1:1)

Relative clauses in Arabic exhibit some interesting syntactic restrictions. The relative pronoun itself, which in the Classical and Modern Standard varieties declines for gender and number (and in the dual, also for case), is an Arabic innovation; the inherited Proto-Semitic forms survive in Arabic only as a determinative pronoun ('the one of'). But the relative pronoun is only used when the antecedent is definite (96). When the antecedent is indefinite, the relative clause is asyndetic (97). This type of asyndetic clause, with an indefinite antecedent in the free (unbound) state, is also found occasionally in Geʿez, Mehri, and elsewhere, though only in Arabic is it the rule.

Modern Standard Arabic

(96)	*ʔas-siyyāḥ-u*	*llaðīna*	*yaṣilūna*
	the-tourists-NOM	REL:M.PL	arrive:NONPAST.3M.PL

'the tourists who arrive'

(97) *rajul-un* *yamtaliku* *š-šajāʕat-a*
man-NOM.INDEF possess:NONPAST.3M.SG the-courage-ACC
'a man who possesses courage' (Ryding 2005)

In modern Arabic dialects, the relative pronoun is usually a single, indeclinable form, but relative clauses exhibit the same distinction based on whether or not the antecedent is definite or indefinite (98–99).

Iraqi (Muslim Baghdadi) Arabic
(98) *l-iḥṣān* *illi* *yiḷab* *haš-šōṭ*
the-horse REL win:PAST.3M.SG this-race
'the horse that won this race'

(99) *ibnayya* *tiḥči* *xamis* *luɣāt*
girl speak:PRES-3F.SG five languages
'a girl who speaks five languages' (Erwin 1963)

When a Semitic relative pronoun stands in a prepositional relationship, a resumptive pronoun is normally employed. In some languages this is optional, but most often it is obligatory (100). Resumptive pronouns are also found even when the relative pronoun stands for the direct object, and in fact, such use of a resumptive pronoun is obligatory in some languages, including many Arabic dialects (101). Only very rarely do we find a preposition preceding a relative pronoun (like English 'in which'); Geʿez is a language in which this is possible, though still very infrequent (102).

Biblical Hebrew
(100) *hā-ʔāreṣ* *ʔăšer* *gar-tā* *b-āh*
the-land[F] REL live:PAST-2M.SG in-3F.SG
'the land in which you lived' (Gen. 21:23)

Egyptian Arabic
(101) *iṛ-ṛāgil* *illi* *šuf-t-u* *imbāriḥ*
the-man REL see:PAST-2M.SG-3M.SG yesterday
'the man that you saw yesterday' (Abdel-Massih et al. 1979)

Ge‘ez
(102) *wark’-a* *ʔams’āʔ-na …* *ba-za* *nəśśāyyat’*
money-ACC bring:PAST-1.PL with-REL buy:NONPAST.1PL
ʔəkl-a
food-ACC
‘We brought money … with which to buy food.’ (Gen. 43:22; Dillmann 1907)

As discussed in §4.1, Proto-Semitic relative clauses followed their antecedents, but in modern Ethiopian Semitic languages, relative clauses precede (50, in §4.1).

4.11 SUBORDINATE CLAUSES

Subordinate clauses in the Semitic languages can be marked either by an explicit conjunction, or, less often, by special syntactic constructions using nominalized verbal forms. We find temporal (103), conditional (104), and causal (105) subordinating conjunctions, among other types.

Omani Mehri
(103) *wəzmōna* *t-īkəm* *fəndēl* *mət*
give:FUT.M.SG ACC-2M.PL sweet.potato.COLL when
nakakəm
come:PAST.2M.PL
‘I will give you sweet potatoes when you come back.’ (Rubin 2010b)

Ge‘ez
(104) *ʔəmma* *nabar-ka* *zəyya* *yərakkəbu-ka*
if stay:PAST-2M.SG here find:FUT.3M.PL-2M.SG
‘If you stay here, they will find you.’ (Tropper 2002a)

Amharic
(105) *səlä-tammämä* *al-mät’t’ä-mm*
because-be.sick:PAST-3M.SG NEG-come:PAST.3M.SG-NEG
‘Because he was sick, he didn’t come.’ (Leslau 1995)

We also find subordinate clauses indicated by means of a preposition plus an infinitive or a verbal noun (106–107).

Biblical Hebrew

(106) *lō yēraʕ ləbāb-əkā bə-titt-əkā*
NEG be.bad:FUT.3M.SG heart-2M.SG PREP-give:INF-2M.SG
l-ō
to-3M.SG
'Your heart will not be grieved when you give to him (lit.: at your giving).' (Deut. 15:10)

Amharic

(107) *mist-u-n bä-mägdäl-u*
wife-3M.SG-ACC PREP-kill:INF-3M.SG
täkässäsä
indict:PASS.PAST.3M.SG
'He was indicted because he killed his wife (lit.: at his killing).' (Leslau 1995)

5 LEXICON

The Semitic languages—at least the classical languages—show a very high proportion of native Semitic roots, with the consequence that the lexicons of the Semitic languages have much in common (Bennett 1998 provides some convenient word-lists). How much the Proto-Semitic lexicon has derived from Afroasiatic is very difficult to determine, since while some of the morphological correspondences between the Afroasiatic branches are reasonably clear, finding regular phonological correspondences has proven very difficult. Therefore, proposed cognates between Semitic and Afroasiatic should always be regarded with a high degree of caution.

As discussed above (§2.3, §3.4), consonantal roots, usually triliteral, form the basis of the Semitic lexicon, since all verbs and nearly all nouns and adjectives are associated with a lexical root. There are, however, a significant number of primary (or isolated) Semitic nouns, which are not associated with a root. Some examples are the Proto-Semitic nouns **ʔax* 'brother', **dam* 'blood', **śapat* 'lip', and **ʔarnab* 'hare' (Fox 2003).

Given the history of the regions in which the Semitic languages are spoken, it should be no surprise that borrowing of vocabulary has been frequent. In many cases, the source of borrowing has been another Semitic language. Akkadian was widely used throughout the Near East for much of the second millennium BCE, and because of this, we find a number of Akkadian loans in Biblical Hebrew (Mankowski 2000) and various dialects of Aramaic (Kaufman 1974). Aramaic itself was also long a dominant language in the region, and numerous Aramaic borrowings or calques are found in Arabic (Retsö 2006), all periods of Hebrew (M. Wagner 1966; Kutscher 1982), and elsewhere. Over the last millennium, Arabic has had heavy lexical influence on the Modern South Arabian group (Lonnet 2009) and on most Neo-Aramaic dialects, and has provided a sizable number of loans to the Ethiopian languages (Leslau 1990; Zaborski 2003).

Influence from non-Semitic languages is found already in Akkadian, which borrowed a large number of nouns (but no verbs) from Sumerian (Lieberman 1977). All other ancient languages possess some non-Semitic vocabulary items, but non-Semitic influence really becomes pervasive in the Hellenistic and Roman periods; Hebrew, Aramaic (especially Syriac), and Ge'ez all have sizable amounts of Greek loanwords (see, e.g., Krauss 1898–99 and Sperber 1984 on Hebrew, and Brock 2007 on Syriac); Arabic has a much smaller, but not insignificant, number of Greek loanwords (Gutas 2007). Large numbers of Persian (usually Middle Persian) loanwords are found in Arabic (Yarshater 1998; Asbaghi 1988) and Aramaic (Ciancaglini 2008). In the modern period, non-Semitic lexical influence is very substantial for a number of languages. All modern Ethiopian Semitic languages have large numbers of Cushitic loans (Leslau 1988), as does Ge'ez, to some extent; many Neo-Aramaic dialects have an abundance of Kurdish loans (Khan 2004, 2008a); Maltese has a copious amount of Italian loans (Aquilina 1976); Moroccan Arabic has scores of French loans (Heath 1989); and Modern Hebrew has countless loans from English. Turkish has provided a fair number of loans into both literary and spoken Arabic, though perhaps less than one would expect, given the centuries of Ottoman dominion over most of the Arab world (Procházka 2004). Studying the lexical inventories of the Semitic languages is really a lesson in the political and cultural history of the Near East.

6 Guide to Further Reading

This section will provide some direction for further research on the Semitic languages. At present, there exists no comprehensive bibliographical work on Semitic. The volumes by Hospers (1973–74) are useful, but well out of date. An extensive online bibliography can be found on the website of the journal *Aula Orientalis* (http://www.telefonica.net/web2/aulaorientalis/).

It will be observed below that several of the standard grammars of Semitic languages date from the late 19th and early 20th centuries. In these cases, I have also provided more recent sources, in addition to these classic, still valuable works.

General Linguistics: As a basic reference for linguistic terminology, Crystal (2008) and Matthews (2007) are very helpful. For an introduction to historical and comparative linguistics, there are several good books available, including Campbell (2004). Akmajian et al. (2010) and O'Grady et al. (2010) are general introductions to the many subfields of linguistics.

Afroasiatic: Very brief sketches of the non-Semitic branches of Afroasiatic can be found in Hayward (2000) and Huehnergard (2004). The classic survey of Afroasiatic is that of Diakonoff (1988). While this work provides useful data, its reconstructions should not be relied upon. Any comparative grammar or dictionary comparing two or more branches of Afroasiatic must be used with great caution.

General Semitic: The standard comparative grammar of Semitic is probably still that of Brockelmann (1908–13), though it is seriously outdated. A number of works have appeared in recent years, though all of these must be used with some caution. Lipiński (2000) and Kienast (2001) are more comprehensive treatments, while Bennett (1998), Stempel (1999), and Haelewyck (2007) are much briefer. Moscati (1964), upon which linguists so often rely, and which focuses mainly on the ancient languages, is outdated. Hetzron (1997), Woodard (2004), and Kaye (1997; 2007) each contain excellent sketches of some of the individual Semitic languages. There is no comparative etymological dictionary of Semitic, though Cohen, Bron, and Lonnet (1994–), with nine fascicles as of 2010 (through the letter *Ḥ*, according to the Hebrew ordering of the alphabet) is quite useful. Leslau (1991) is an etymological dictionary of Geʿez, but it has an index of Semitic roots that makes it a partial substitute for a Semitic etymological dictionary. Militarev and Kogan (2000; 2005) treat only limited semantic fields.

Akkadian and Eblaite: The standard grammar of Akkadian is that of von Soden (2005). The textbook of Huehnergard (2005b), which focuses mainly on Old Babylonian, is comprehensive enough to be used as a basic reference grammar for most purposes, and is superior to von Soden in its clarity and in its treatment of certain morphological and syntactic features. Hasselbach (2005) is a treatment of Old Akkadian, and Hämeen-Anttila (2000) is a useful work devoted to Neo-Assyrian. A lengthy overview of both Akkadian and Eblaite can be found in Huehnergard and Woods (2004).

Modern South Arabian: Relatively little has been published on the Modern South Arabian languages. A number of grammatical studies were published in the first two decades of the 20th century (see Leslau 1946 and Rubin 2010b for details), but from the rest of the 20th century we have only the syntactical study of E. Wagner (1953) and a few brief grammatical sketches (e.g., Johnstone 1975; Simeone-Senelle 1997; Lonnet 2006). A comprehensive grammar of Mehri, the most widely spoken language of this group, was published in 2010 (Rubin 2010b).

Ethiopian Semitic: For Geʿez, the classical language of Ethiopia, the standard and most comprehensive reference grammar is that of Dillmann (1907). A more concise, but still very useful grammar was recently published by Tropper (2002a). Lambdin (1978) is a textbook, but is very valuable; in fact, a good amount of the information in Tropper's reference grammar seems to have come from Lambdin. There are grammars published for many, though not all, of the modern Ethiopian Semitic languages. Leslau (1995) is the standard for

Amharic, and is an outstanding reference. Leslau has also published grammars, or at least grammatical sketches, for many other Ethiopian languages (e.g., Tigrinya, 1941; Tigré, 1945b; Argobba, 1997; Zay, 1999). Detailed grammars of two Gurage languages have recently been published by Meyer (Zay, 2005; Wolane, 2006). For Tigrinya, the second most widely spoken modern Ethiopian language, there is no recent, comprehensive grammar, though Melles (2001) is a useful short treatment. Raz (1983) is a brief grammar of Tigré. The encyclopedia of Uhlig et al. (2003–), with three of the planned six volumes published (as of 2010), is an excellent reference for all things Ethiopian, including the languages.

Arabic: For a general overview of the various periods of Arabic, see Versteegh (1997) and Ferrando (2001). The standard grammar of Classical Arabic is still that of Wright (1896–98), though the smaller grammar of Fischer (2002) is also useful. On Middle Arabic, Lentin (2008) is a good place to start. Blau (1966–67; 1988; 1999) are also excellent sources. For Modern Standard Arabic, there are a number of very good recent reference grammars, including Ryding (2005) and Mace (1998). The study of modern Arabic dialects is a vast field. Three good handbooks, which provide some overview of the dialects, are those of Fischer and Jastrow (1980), Behnstedt and Woidich (2005), and Corriente and Vicente (2008). Excellent sketches of the dialects, as well as a wide variety of other articles on other Arabic topics, can be found in the recent encyclopedia edited by Versteegh et al. (2006–09). A number of fine Arabic dialect grammars are also published in the series *Semitica Viva*, published by Harrassowitz. On Arabic-based creoles, see Owens (1997; 2006) and Wellens (2005). On the Ancient North Arabian inscriptional dialects, see Macdonald (2000; 2004).

Ṣayhadic (Old South Arabian): The only Ṣayhadic language described at length is Sabaic (also called Sabaean), the phonology and morphology of which are treated in the grammar of Stein (2003). On the stick and palm-leaf texts (also discussed in Stein 2003), see Ryckmans, Müller, and Abdallah (1994) and Stein (2005; 2010). Brief sketches of the other languages of the Ṣayhadic group can be found in Beeston (1984) and in Nebes and Stein (2004).

Ugaritic, Sam'alian, and Deir 'Allā: Tropper (2000a) is a comprehensive grammar of Ugaritic that has become the standard reference work. The same author also published a much abridged version (2002b), which is also very useful. Watson and Wyatt (1999) is a very useful volume for Ugaritic Studies in general. On the Sam'alian texts, see Tropper (1993), and on the text from Deir 'Allā, see the collection of articles in Hoftijzer and van der Kooij (1991).

Hebrew and Canaanite: The most widely referenced grammar of Biblical Hebrew in English is still that of Kautzsch (1910), though it is a century old. Another widely used grammar, which is more recent, is that of Joüon and Muraoka (2008). For Rabbinic Hebrew, Pérez-Fernández (1999) is a decent introduction; Segal (1927) is useful, but outdated. For Qumran Hebrew, see Qimron (1986). For Modern Hebrew, the most comprehensive grammar is that of Glinert (1989). The more recent works by Coffin and Bolozky (2005) and Glinert (2005), though intended more for students, are also very useful. For a general overview of the history of Hebrew, Kutscher (1982) and Sáenz-Badillos (1993) are very good sources. A multi-volume encyclopedia on the Hebrew language is in production (Khan et al. forthcoming), and this is sure to become a major reference work. For Phoenician, the standard reference grammar is that of Friedrich and Röllig (1999), though Hackett (2004) provides a nice sketch of the language. For the Canaanite of the Tell El-Amarna tablets, see Rainey (1996).

Aramaic: As discussed above (§1.9), Aramaic is the cover term for a large number of languages and dialects. Among the many reference grammars focusing on the ancient dialects, we can cite just a few: Degen (1969) on Old Aramaic; Folmer (1995) and Muraoka and Porten (2003) on Imperial Aramaic; Dalman (1905) on various Jewish dialects; Nöldeke (1904) on Syriac; Müller-Kessler (1991) on Christian Palestinian Aramaic; and Macuch (1965) on Mandaic. A wonderful historical overview of the Aramaic family can be found in Brock (2001). Another handy overview of Aramaic, with grammatical sketches and many bibliographical references, is Ferrer (2004). Brock (2006) is an exellent guide to Syriac studies. The study of Modern Aramaic (Neo-Aramaic) has exploded in the last two decades, and there are now excellent grammars of numerous Neo-Aramaic languages. For NENA, noteworthy are those of Khan (1999, 2002, 2004, 2008a, 2008b, 2009); for Turoyo, see Jastrow (1985); for Neo-West Aramaic, see Arnold (1989–91); and for Neo-Mandaic, see Häberl (2009). There are also more than a dozen volumes (by various authors) devoted to Neo-Aramaic in the series *Semitica Viva*, published by Harrassowitz. A very nice overview of the many NENA dialects can be found in Khan (2007).

BIBLIOGRAPHY

Abdel-Massih, Ernest T., Zaki N. Abdel-Malek, and El-Said M. Badawi. 1979. *A Comprehensive Study of Egyptian Arabic. Volume 3: A Reference Grammar of Egyptian Arabic*. Ann Arbor: Center for Near Eastern and African Studies, The University of Michigan.

Abu-Haidar, Farida. 1991. *Christian Arabic of Baghdad*. Wiesbaden: Harrassowitz.

Akmajian, Adrian, et al. 2010. *Linguistics: An Introduction to Language and Communication*. 6th edn. Cambridge, MA: The MIT Press.

Ambros, Arne. 1998. *Bonġornu, Kif Int? Einführung in die maltesische Sprache*. Wiesbaden: Ludwig Reichert.

Appleyard, David L. 2004. Some Thoughts on the Origin of the Amharic Object Marker -[ə]*n*. In *Studia Aethiopica: In Honour of Siegbert Uhlig on the Occasion of his 65th Birthday*, ed. Verena Böll et al., pp. 291–301. Wiesbaden: Harrassowitz.

Aquilina, Joseph. 1976. *Maltese Linguistic Surveys*. Msida, Malta: University of Malta.

Arnold, Werner. 1989–91. *Das Neuwestaramäische*. 5 vols. Wiesbaden: Harrassowitz.

Aro, Jussi. 1977. Pronunciation of the "Emphatic" Consonants in Semitic Languages. *Studia Orientalia* 47:5–18.

Asbaghi, Asya. 1988. *Persische Lehnwörter im Arabischen*. Wiesbaden: Harrassowitz.

Bar-Asher, Elitzur A. 2007. The Origin and Typology of the Pattern *Qtil li* in Syriac and Babylonian Aramaic. [In Hebrew.] In *Sha'arei Lashon: Studies in Hebrew, Aramaic, and Jewish Languages Presented to Moshe Bar-Asher*, ed. A. Maman, S.E. Fassberg, and Y. Breuer, Vol. 2, pp. 360–92. Jerusalem: Bialik Institute.

Beeston, A.F.L. 1984. *Sabaic Grammar*. Manchester: Journal of Semitic Studies.

_____. 1987. Apologia for "Sayhadic". *Proceedings of the Seminar for Arabian Studies* 17:13–14. (Reprinted with updated bibliography in *A.F.L. Beeston at the Arabian Seminar and Other Papers*, ed. M.C.A. Macdonald and C.S. Phillips, pp. 79–80. Oxford: Archaeopress, 2005.)

Behnstedt, Peter, and Manfred Woidich. 2005. *Arabische Dialektgeographie: Eine Einführung*. Leiden: Brill.

Bennett, Patrick R. 1998. *Comparative Semitic Linguistics: A Manual*. Winona Lake, IN: Eisenbrauns.

Blanc, Haim. 1964. *Communal Dialects of Baghdad*. Cambridge, MA: Harvard University Press.

Blau, Joshua. 1966–67. *A Grammar of Christian Arabic Based Mainly on South-Palestinian Texts from the First Millennium*. 3 vols. Leuven: Peeters.

_____. 1988. *Studies in Middle Arabic and Its Judaeo-Arabic Variety*. Jerusalem: Magnes.

_____. 1999. *The Emergence and Linguistic Background of Judaeo-Arabic*. 3d edn. Jerusalem: Ben Zvi Institute.

Brock, Sebastian P. 2001. *The Hidden Pearl: The Syrian Orthodox Church and Its Ancient Aramaic Heritage*. 3 vols. With the assistance of David G.K. Taylor. Rome: Trans World Films Italia.

_____. 2006. *An Introduction to Syriac Studies*. Piscataway, NJ: Gorgias.

_____. 2007. Greek and Syriac. In *A History of Ancient Greek: From the Beginnings to Late Antiquity*, ed. A.-F. Christidis, pp. 819–26. Cambridge: Cambridge University Press.

Brockelmann, Carl. 1908–13. *Grundriss der vergleichenden Grammatik der semitischen Sprachen*. 2 vols. Berlin: von Reuther.

Brustad, Kristen E. 2000. *The Syntax of Spoken Arabic: A Comparative Study of Moroccan, Egyptian, Syrian, and Kuwaiti Dialects*. Washington, DC: Georgetown University Press.

Butts, Aaron Michael. 2010. The Etymology and Derivation of the Syriac Adverbial Ending -ɔʾiθ. *Journal of Near Eastern Studies* 69:79–86.

Campbell, Lyle. 2004. *Historical Linguistics: An Introduction*. 2d edn. Cambridge, MA: The MIT Press.

Ciancaglini, Claudia A. 2008. *Iranian Loanwords in Syriac*. Wiesbaden: Ludwig Reichert.

Coffin, Edna Amir, and Shmuel Bolozky. 2005. *A Reference Grammar of Modern Hebrew*. Cambridge: Cambridge University Press.

Cohen, David. [1984] 2003. *La phrase nominale et l'évolution du système verbal en sémitique: Études de syntaxe historique*. Leuven: Peeters.

Cohen, David, François Bron, and Antoine Lonnet. 1994–. *Dictionnaire des racines sémitiques, ou attestées dans les langues sémitiques*. Leuven: Peeters.

Cook, John A. 2006. The Finite Verbal Forms in Biblical Hebrew Do Express Aspect. *Journal of the Ancient Near Eastern Society* 30:21–35.

Corriente, Federico, and Ángeles Vicente, eds. 2008. *Manual de dialectología neoárabe*. Zaragoza: Instituto de Estudios Islámicos y del Oriente Próximo.

Cowell, Mark W. 1964. *A Reference Grammar of Syrian Arabic*. Washington, DC: Georgetown University Press.

Crystal, David. 2008. *A Dictionary of Linguistics and Phonetics*. 6th edn. Oxford: Wiley-Blackwell.

Dalman, Gustaf H. [1905] 1960. *Grammatik des jüdisch-palästinischen Aramäisch*. 2d edn. Leipzig: J.C. Hinrichs. Reprint, Darmstadt: Wissenschaftliche Buchgesellschaft.

Degen, Rainer. 1969. *Altaramäische Grammatik*. Wiesbaden: Franz Steiner.

Deutscher, Guy. 2000. Stability Against the Odds? The Survival of Verb Final Order in Akkadian. In *Stability, Change and Variation in Word-Order Patterns over Time*, ed. Rosanna Sornicola, Erich Poppe, and Ariel Shisha-Halevy, pp. 55–69. Amsterdam and Philadelphia: John Benjamins.

Diakonoff, I.M. 1988. *Afrasian Languages*. Moscow: Nauka.

Diem, Werner. 1982. Die Entwicklung des Derivationsmorphems der *t*-Stämme im Semitischen. *Zeitschrift der Deutschen Morgenländischen Gesellschaft* 132:29–84.

Dillmann, August. [1907] 1974. *Ethiopic Grammar*. 2d edn. Revised and edited by Carl Bezold. Translated by James A. Crichton. London: Williams & Norgate. Reprint, Amsterdam: Philo.

Erwin, Wallace M. 1963. *A Short Reference Grammar of Iraqi Arabic*. Washington, DC: Georgetown University Press.

Faber, Alice. 1981. Phonetic Reconstruction. *Glossa* 15:233–62.

_____. 1985. Akkadian Evidence for Proto-Semitic Affricates. *Journal of Cuneiform Studies* 37:101–7.

Fassberg, Steven E. 1999. The Lengthened Imperative קָטְלָה in Biblical Hebrew. *Hebrew Studies* 40:7–13.

Ferrer, Joan. 2004. *Esbozo de historia de la lengua aramea*. Cordoba: Servicio de Publicaciones de la Universidad de Córdoba.

Ferrando, Ignacio. 2001. *Introducción a la historia de la lengua arabe: Nuevas perspectivas*. Zaragoza: Navarro & Navarro.

Fischer, Wolfdietrich. 2002. *A Grammar of Classical Arabic*. 3d edn. Translated by Jonathan Rodgers. New Haven: Yale University Press.

Fischer, Wolfdietrich, and Otto Jastrow, eds. 1980. *Handbuch der arabischen Dialekte*. Wiesbaden: Harrassowitz.

Folmer, M.L. 1995. *The Aramaic Language in the Achaemenid Period: A Study in Linguistic Variation*. Leuven: Peeters.

Fox, Joshua. 2003. *Semitic Noun Patterns*. Winona Lake, IN: Eisenbrauns.

Friedrich, Johannes, and Wolfgang Röllig. 1999. *Phönizisch-Punische Grammatik*. 3d edn. Revised by Maria G. Amadasi Guzzo. Rome: Pontificio Istituto Biblico.

Gensler, Orin D. 1997. Reconstructing Quadriliteral Verb Inflection: Ethiopic, Akkadian, Proto-Semitic. *Journal of Semitic Studies* 42:229–57.

_______. 2000. Why Semitic Adverbializers (Akkadian *-iš*, Syriac *-ā'īṯ*) Should Not Be Derived from Existential **'īṯ*. *Journal of Semitic Studies* 45:233–65.

Glinert, Lewis. 1989. *The Grammar of Modern Hebrew*. Cambridge: Cambridge University Press.

_____. 2005. *Modern Hebrew: An Essential Grammar*. 3d edn. New York and London: Routledge.

Greenberg, Joseph. 1950. The Patterning of Root Morphemes in Semitic. *Word* 6:162–81.

Gutas, Dimitri. 2007. Greek Loanwords. In *Encyclopedia of Arabic Language and Linguistics, Volume II*, ed. Kees Versteegh et al., pp. 198–202. Leiden: Brill.

Häberl, Charles G. 2009. *The Neo-Mandaic Dialect of Khorramshahr*. Wiesbaden: Harrassowitz.

Hackett, Jo Ann. 2004. Phoenician and Punic. In *Cambridge Encyclopedia of the World's Ancient Languages*, ed. Roger Woodard, pp. 365–85. Cambridge: Cambridge University Press.

Haelewyck, Jean-Claude. 2007. *Grammaire comparée des langues sémitiques*. Brussels: Safran.

Hämeen-Anttila, Jaakko. 2000. *A Sketch of Neo-Assyrian Grammar*. Helsinki: Neo-Assyrian Text Corpus Project of the University of Helsinki.

Hasselbach, Rebecca. 2005. *Sargonic Akkadian: A Historical and Comparative Study of the Syllabic Texts*. Wiesbaden: Harrassowitz.

_____. 2006. The Ventive/Energic in Semitic – A Morphological Study. *Zeitschrift der Deutschen Morgenländischen Gesellschaft* 156:309–28.

Hayward, Richard J. 2000. Afroasiatic. In *African Languages: An Introduction*, ed. Bernd Heine and Derek Nurse, pp. 74–98. Cambridge: Cambridge University Press.

Heath, Jeffrey. 1989. *From Code-Switching to Borrowing: Foreign and Diglossic Mixing in Moroccan Arabic*. London: Kegan Paul International.

Hetzron, Robert. 1967. Agaw Numerals and Incongruence in Semitic. *Journal of Semitic Studies* 12:169–97.

_____. 1972. *Ethiopian Semitic: Studies in Classification*. Manchester: Manchester University Press.

_____. 1974. La division des langues sémitiques. In *Actes du Premier Congrès International de Linguistique Sémitique et Chamito-Sémitque, Paris 16–19 juillet, 1969*, ed. André Caquot and David Cohen, pp. 181–94. The Hague and Paris: Mouton.

_____. 1976. Two Principles of Genetic Reconstruction. *Lingua* 38:89–108.

_____, ed. 1997. *The Semitic Languages*. London: Routledge.

Hoberman, Robert D., and Mark Aronoff. 2003. The Verbal Morphology of Maltese: From Semitic to Romance. In *Language Processing and Acquisition in Languages of Semitic, Root-Based, Morphology*, ed. Joseph Shimron, pp. 61–78. Amsterdam and Philadelphia: John Benjamins.

Hoftijzer, J. and G. van der Kooij, eds. 1991. *The Balaam Text from Deir 'Alla Re-evaluated. Proceedings of the International Symposium held at Leiden 21–24 August 1989*. Leiden: Brill.

Hospers, J.H. 1973–74. *A Basic Bibliography for the Study of the Semitic Languages*. 2 vols. Leiden: Brill.

Huehnergard, John. 1983. Asseverative **la* and Hypothetical **lu/law* in Semitic. *Journal of the American Oriental Society* 103:569–93.

_____. 1987a. Three Notes on Akkadian Morphology. In *"Working With No Data": Semitic and Egyptian Studies Presented to Thomas O. Lambdin*, ed. David M. Golomb, pp. 181–93. Winona Lake, IN: Eisenbrauns.

_____. 1987b. "Stative," Predicative Form, Pseudo-Verb. *Journal of Near Eastern Studies* 46:215–32.

_____. 1991. Remarks on the Classification of the Northwest Semitic Languages. In *The Balaam Text from Deir 'Alla Re-evaluated. Proceedings of the International Symposium held at Leiden 21–24 August 1989*, ed. J. Hoftijzer and G. van der Kooij, pp. 282–93. Leiden: Brill.

_____. 2003. Akkadian ḫ and West Semitic ḥ. In *Orientalia: Papers of the Oriental Institute 3* (*Studia Semitica*), ed. Leonid Kogan, pp. 102–19. Moscow: Russian State University for the Humanities.

_____. 2004. Afro-Asiatic. In *Cambridge Encyclopedia of the World's Ancient Languages*, ed. Roger Woodard, pp. 138–59. Cambridge: Cambridge University Press.

_____. 2005a. Features of Central Semitic. In *Biblical and Oriental Essays in Memory of William L. Moran*, ed. Agustinus Gianto, pp. 155–203. Rome: Pontificio Istituto Biblico.

_____. 2005b. *A Grammar of Akkadian*. 2d edn. Winona Lake, IN: Eisenbrauns.

_____. 2006a. On the Etymology of the Hebrew Relative *šɛ-*. In *Biblical Hebrew in Its Northwest Semitic Setting: Typological and Historical Perspectives*, ed. Steven E. Fassberg and Avi Hurvitz, pp. 103–125. Jerusalem: Magnes.

_____. 2006b. Proto-Semitic and Proto-Akkadian. In *The Akkadian Language in its Semitic Context*, ed. G. Deutscher and N.J.C. Kouwenberg, pp. 1–18. Leiden: Nederlands Instituut voor het Nabije Oosten.

Huehnergard, John, and Christopher Woods. 2004. Akkadian and Eblaite. In *Cambridge Encyclopedia of the World's Ancient Languages*, ed. Roger Woodard, pp. 218–87. Cambridge: Cambridge University Press.

Johnstone, T.M. 1975. The Modern South Arabian Languages. *Afroasiatic Linguistics* 1:93–121.

Jastrow, Otto. 1985. *Laut- und Formenlehre des neuaramäischen Dialekts von Mīdin im Ṭūr 'Abdīn*. 3d edn. Wiesbaden: Harrassowitz.

Joosten, Jan. 1998. The Functions of the Semitic D stem: Biblical Hebrew Materials for a Comparative-Historical Approach. *Orientalia* 67:202–30.

_____. 2002. Do the Finite Verbal Forms in Biblical Hebrew Express Aspect? *Journal of the Ancient Near Eastern Society* 29:49–70.

Joüon, Paul, and T. Muraoka. 2008. *A Grammar of Biblical Hebrew*. 2d edn. Rome: Pontificio Istituto Biblico.

Jullien de Pommerol, Patrice. 1999. *Grammaire pratique de l'arabe tchadien*. Paris: Karthala.

Kaufman, Stephen A. 1974. *The Akkadian Influences on Aramaic*. Chicago: The University of Chicago Press.

Kautzsch, E., ed. 1910. *Gesenius' Hebrew Grammar*. 2d edn. Revised and translated by A.E. Cowley. Oxford: Clarendon.

Kaye, Alan. 1997. *Phonologies of Asia and Africa*. 2 vols. Winona Lake, IN: Eisenbrauns.

_____. 2007. *Morphologies of Asia and Africa*. 2 vols. Winona Lake, IN: Eisenbrauns.

Khan, Geoffrey. 1999. *A Grammar of Neo-Aramaic: The Dialect of the Jews of Arbel*. Leiden: Brill.

_____. 2002. *The Neo-Aramaic Dialect of Qaraqosh*. Leiden: Brill.

_____. 2004. *The Jewish Neo-Aramaic Dialect of Sulemaniyya and Ḥalabja*. Leiden: Brill.

_____. 2007. The North-Eastern Neo-Aramaic Dialects. *Journal of Semitic Studies* 52:1–20.

_____. 2008a. *The Neo-Aramaic Dialect of Barwar*. 3 vols. Leiden: Brill.

_____. 2008b. *The Jewish Neo-Aramaic Dialect of Urmi*. Piscataway, NJ: Gorgias.

_____. 2009. *The Jewish Neo-Aramaic Dialect of Sanandaj*. Piscataway, NJ: Gorgias.

Khan, Geoffrey, et al., eds. Forthcoming. *Encyclopedia of Hebrew Language and Linguistics*. Leiden: Brill.

Kienast, Burkhart. 2001. *Historische Semitische Sprachwissenschaft*. Wiesbaden: Harrassowitz.

Kouwenberg, N.J.C. 1997. *Gemination in the Akkadian Verb*. Assen: Van Gorcum.

_____. 2003. Evidence for Post-Glottalized Consonants in Assyrian. *Journal of Cuneiform Studies* 55:75–86.

Krauss, Samuel. [1898–99] 1987. *Griechische und lateinische Lehnwörter im Talmud, Midrasch, und Targum*. 2 vols. Berlin: S. Calvary. Reprint, Hildesheim: Olms.

Kuryłowicz, Jerzy. 1973. *Studies in Semitic Metrics and Grammar*. London: Curzon.

Kutscher, E.Y. 1969. Two 'Passive' Constructions in Aramaic in the Light of Persian. In *Proceedings of the International Conference on Semitic Studies Held in Jerusalem, 19–23 July, 1965*, pp. 132–51. Jerusalem: Israel Academy of Sciences and Humanities.

_____. 1982. *A History of the Hebrew Language*. Ed. Raphael Kutscher. Jerusalem: Magnes.

Lambdin, Thomas O. 1978. *Introduction to Classical Ethiopic (Ge'ez)*. Atlanta: Scholars.

Lentin, Jérôme. 2008. Middle Arabic. In *Encyclopedia of Arabic Language and Linguistics, Volume III*, ed. Kees Versteegh et al., pp. 215–24. Leiden: Brill.

Leslau, Wolf. 1941. *Documents tigrinya (Éthiopien septentrionel): Grammaire et textes*. Paris: C. Klincksieck.

_____. 1945a. The Influence of Cushitic on the Semitic Languages of Ethiopia: A Problem of Substratum. *Word* 1:59–82.

_____. 1945b. *Short Grammar of Tigré*. New Haven: American Oriental Society.

_____. 1946. Bibliography of the Modern South Arabic Languages. *Bulletin of the New York Public Library* 50:607–33.

_____. 1988. Analysis of the Ge'ez Vocabulary: Ge'ez and Cushitic. *Rassegna di Studi Etiopici* 32:60–109.

_____. 1990. *Arabic Loanwords in Ethiopian Semitic*. Wiesbaden: Harrassowitz.

_____. 1991. *Comparative Dictionary of Ge'ez (Classical Ethiopic)*. Wiesbaden: Harrassowitz.

_____. 1995. *Reference Grammar of Amharic*. Wiesbaden: Harrassowitz.

_____. 1997. *Ethiopic Documents: Argobba. Grammar and Dictionary*. Wiesbaden: Harrassowitz.

_____. 1999. *Zway Ethiopic Documents: Grammar and Dictionary*. Wiesbaden: Harrassowitz.

Lieberman, Stephen J. 1977. *The Sumerian Loanwords in Old-Babylonian Akkadian*. Missoula, MT: Scholars.

_____. 1986. The Afro-Asiatic Background of the Semitic N-Stem: Toward the Origins of the Stem-Afformatives of the Semitic and Afro-Asiatic Verb. *Bibliotheca Orientalia* 43:577–628.

Lipiński, Edward. 2000. *Semitic Languages: Outline of a Comparative Grammar*. 2d edn. Leuven: Peeters.

Lonnet, Antoine. 1998. Le Socotri: une métamorphose contrariée. In *Actes du 1er congrès Chamito-Sémitique de Fès*, ed. Mohamed El Medlaoui et al., pp. 69–85. Fes: Faculté des Lettres et des Sciences Humaines Saïs-Fès.

_____. 2006. Les langues sudarabiques modernes. *Faits de Langues* 2:27–44.

_____. 2009. South Arabian, Modern. In *Encyclopedia of Arabic Language and Linguistics, Volume IV*, ed. Kees Versteegh et al., pp. 296–300. Leiden: Brill.

Macdonald, M.C.A. 2000. Reflections on the Linguistic Map of Pre-Islamic Arabia. *Arabian Archaeology and Epigraphy* 11: 28–79.

_____. 2004. Ancient North Arabian. In *Cambridge Encyclopedia of the World's Ancient Languages*, ed. Roger Woodard, pp. 488–533. Cambridge: Cambridge University Press.

Mace, John. 1998. *Arabic Grammar: A Reference Guide*. Edinburgh: Edinburgh University Press.

Macuch, Rudolf. 1965. *Handbook of Classical and Modern Mandaic*. Berlin: de Gruyter.

Mankowski, Paul V. 2000. *Akkadian Loanwords in Biblical Hebrew*. Winona Lake, IN: Eisenbrauns.

Matthews, P.H. 2007. *The Concise Oxford Dictionary of Linguistics*. 2d edn. Oxford: Oxford University Press.

Melles, Mulugeta Girmay. 2001. *Tigrinya Grammar and Reader*. Springfield, VA: Dunwoody.

Meyer, Ronny. 2005. *Das Zay: Deskriptive Grammatik einer Ostguragesprache (Äthiosemitisch)*. Cologne: Rüdiger Köppe.

_____. 2006. *Wolane: Descriptive Grammar of an East Gurage Language (Ethiosemitic)*. Cologne: Rüdiger Köppe.

Militarev, Alexander, and Leonid Kogan. 2000. *Semitic Etymological Dictionary. Vol. I: Anatomy of Man and Animals*. Münster: Ugarit-Verlag.

_____. 2005. *Semitic Etymological Dictionary. Vol. II: Animal Names*. Münster: Ugarit-Verlag.

Moscati, Sabatino, ed. 1964. *An Introduction to the Comparative Grammar of the Semitic Languages*. Wiesbaden: Harrassowitz.

Müller-Kessler, Christa. 1991. *Grammatik des christlich-palästinisch-Aramäischen. Teil 1: Schriftlehre, Lautlehre, Formenlehre*. Hildesheim: Olms.

Muraoka, Takamitsu, and Bezalel Porten. 2003. *A Grammar of Egyptian Aramaic*. 2d edn. Leiden: Brill.

Nebes, Norbert, and Peter Stein. 2004. Epigraphic South Arabian. In *Cambridge Encyclopedia of the World's Ancient Languages*, ed. Roger Woodard, pp. 454–87. Cambridge: Cambridge University Press.

Nöldeke, Theodor. [1904] 2001. *Compendious Syriac Grammar*. 2d edn. Translated by James A. Crichton. London: Williams and Norgate. Reprint, Winona Lake, IN: Eisenbrauns.

O'Grady, William, et al. 2010. *Contemporary Linguistics: An Introduction*. 6th edn. Boston: Bedford/St. Martins.

Owens, Jonathan. 1997. Arabic-based Pidgins and Creoles. In *Contact Languages: A Wider Perspective*, ed. Sarah G. Thomason, pp. 125–72. Amsterdam and Philadelphia: John Benjamins.

_____. 2006. Creole Arabic. In *Encyclopedia of Arabic Language and Linguistics, Volume I*, ed. Kees Versteegh et al., pp. 518–26. Leiden: Brill.

Pérez-Fernández, Miguel. 1999. *An Introductory Grammar of Rabbinic Hebrew*. Translated by John Elwolde. Leiden: Brill.

Procházka, Stephen. 2004. The Turkish Contribution to the Arabic Lexicon. In *Linguistic Convergence and Areal Diffusion: Case Studies from Iranian, Semitic, and Turkic*, ed. Éva Ágnes

Csató, Bo Isaksson, and Carina Jahani, pp. 191–202. London and New York: RoutledgeCurzon.

Qimron, Elisha. 1986. *The Hebrew of the Dead Sea Scrolls*. Atlanta: Scholars.

Rainey, Anson F. 1996. *Canaanite in the Amarna Tablets*. 4 vols. Leiden: Brill.

Raz, Shlomo. 1983. *Tigre Grammar and Texts*. Malibu, CA: Undena.

Rendsburg, Gary A. 2003a. A Comprehensive Guide to Israelian Hebrew. *Orient* 38:5–35.

_____. 2003b. The Geographical and Historical Background of the Mishnaic Hebrew Lexicon. *Orient* 38:105–15.

Retsö, Jan. 1983. *The Finite Passive Voice in Modern Arabic Dialects*. Göteborg: Acta Universitatis Gothoburgensis.

_____. 2006. Aramaic/Syriac Loanwords. In *Encyclopedia of Arabic Language and Linguistics, Volume I*, ed. Kees Versteegh et al., pp. 178–82. Leiden: Brill.

Roller, Duane W. 2010. *Eratosthenes' Geography*. Princeton: Princeton University Press.

Rubin, Aaron. 2004a. An Outline of Comparative Egypto-Semitic Morphology. In *Egyptian and Semito-Hamitic (Afro-Asiatic) Studies in Memoriam Werner Vycichl*, ed. Gábor Takács, pp. 454–86. Leiden: Brill.

_____. 2004b. Notes on the Genitive Exponents of Some Modern Arabic Dialects. *Folia Orientalia* 40:327–37.

_____. 2005. *Studies in Semitic Grammaticalization*. Winona Lake, IN: Eisenbrauns.

_____. 2008. The Subgrouping of the Semitic Languages. *Language and Linguistics Compass* 2:61–84.

_____. 2010a. The Development of the Amharic Definite Article and an Indonesian Parallel. *Journal of Semitic Studies* 55:103–14.

_____. 2010b. *The Mehri Language of Oman*. Leiden: Brill.

Ryckmans, Jacques, Walter W. Müller, and Yusuf M. Abdallah. 1994. *Textes du Yémen antique inscrits sur bois (with an English Summary)*. Louvain-la-Neuve: Institut Orientaliste.

Ryding, Karin C. 2005. *A Reference Grammar of Modern Standard Arabic*. Cambridge: Cambridge University Press.

Sáenz-Badillos, Angel. 1993. *A History of the Hebrew Language*. Translated by John Elwolde. Cambridge: Cambridge University Press.

Segal, M.H. 1927. *A Grammar of Mishnaic Hebrew*. Oxford: Clarendon.

Simeone-Senelle, Marie-Claude. 1997. The Modern South Arabian Languages. In *The Semitic Languages*, ed. R. Hetzron, pp. 378–423. London: Routledge.

_____. 2006. Some Characteristics of Dahalik: A Newly Discovered Afro-Semitic Language Spoken in Eritrea. In *Proceedings of the XVth International Conference of Ethiopian Studies, Hamburg, July 20–25, 2003*, ed. Siegbert Uhlig et al., pp. 861–69. Wiesbaden: Harrassowitz.

von Soden, Wolfram. 1995. *Grundriss der akkadischen Grammatik*. 3d edn. With the assistance of W. Meyer. Rome: Pontificio Istituto Biblico.

Speiser, E.A. 1952. The "Elative" in West-Semitic and Akkadian. *Journal of Cuneiform Studies* 6:81–92.

Sperber, Daniel. 1984. *A Dictionary of Greek and Latin Legal Terms in Rabbinic Literature*. Ramat Gan: Bar-Ilan University Press.

Stein, Peter. 2003. *Untersuchungen zur Phonologie und Morphologie des Sabäischen*. Rahden, Westfalia: Marie Leidorf.

_____. 2004. Zur Dialektgeographie des Sabäischen. *Journal of Semitic Studies* 49:225–45.

_____. 2005. The Ancient South Arabian Miniscule Inscriptions on Wood: A New Genre of Pre-Islamic Epigraphy. *Jaarbericht van het vooraziatisch-egyptisch genootschap Ex Oriente Lux* 39:181–99.

_____. 2010. *Die altsüdarabischen Minuskelinschriften auf Holzstäbchen aus der Bayerischen Staatsbibliothek in München. Band 1: Die Inschriften der mittel- und spätsabäischen Periode*. Tübingen and Berlin: Wasmuth.

Steiner, Richard C. 1977. *The Case for Fricative-Laterals in Proto-Semitic*. New Haven: American Oriental Society.

Stempel, Reinhard. 1999. *Abriß einer historischen Grammatik der semitischen Sprachen*. Frankfurt am Main: Peter Lang.

Testen, David. 1985. The Significance of Aramaic *r* < **n*. *Journal of Near Eastern Studies* 44:143–46.

_____. 1993. The East Semitic Precative Paradigm. *Journal of Semitic Studies* 38:1–13.

_____. 1995. Secondary Vowels in Semitic and the Plural Pronominal Endings. In *Kuryłowicz Memorial Volume, Part One*, ed. Wojciech Smoczyński, pp. 543–51. Krakow: Universitas.

Tropper, Josef. 1993. *Die Inschriften von Zincirli*. Münster: Ugarit-Verlag.

_____. 2000a. *Ugaritische Grammatik*. Münster: Ugarit-Verlag.

_____. 2000b. Der altäthiopische Status constructus auf *-a* auf sprachvergleichender Sicht. *Wiener Zeitschrift für die Kunde des Morgenlandes* 90:201–18.

_____. 2002a. *Altäthiopisch: Grammatik des Ge'ez mit Übungstexten und Glossar*. Münster: Ugarit-Verlag.

_____. 2002b. *Ugaritisch: Kurzgefasste Grammatik mit Übungstexten und Glossar*. Münster: Ugarit-Verlag.

Uhlig, Siegbert, et al. 2003–. *Encyclopaedia Aethiopica*. 6 vols. Wiesbaden: Harrassowitz.

Versteegh, Kees. 1997. *The Arabic Language*. Edinburgh: Edinburgh University Press.

Versteegh, Kees, et al., eds. 2006–09. *Encyclopedia of Arabic Language and Linguistics*. 5 vols. Leiden: Brill.

Voigt, Rainer. 1987. Die Personalpronomina der 3. Personen im Semitischen. *Welt des Orients* 18:49–63.

Wagner, Ewald. 1952. Die erste Person Dualis im Semitischen. *Zeitschrift der Deutschen Morgenländischen Gesellschaft* 102:229–33.

_____. 1953. *Syntax der Mehri-Sprache unter Berücksichtigung auch der anderen neusüdarabischen Sprachen*. Berlin: Akademie-Verlag.

Wagner, Max. 1966. *Die lexicalischen und grammaticalischen Aramaismen im alttestamentlichen Hebräisch*. Berlin: Alfred Töpelmann.

Waltisberg, Michael. 2002. Zur Ergativitätshypothese im Semitischen. *Zeitschrift der Deutschen Morgenländischen Gesellschaft* 152:11–62.

Watson, Janet C.E., Bonnie Glover Stalls, Khalid al-Razihi, and Shelagh Weir. 2006. The Language of Jabal Rāziḥ: Arabic or Something Else? *Proceedings of the Seminar for Arabian Studies* 36:35–41.

Watson, Wifred G.E., and Nicolas Wyatt, eds. 1999. *Handbook of Ugaritic Studies*. Leiden: Brill.

Wellens, Ineke. 2005. *The Nubi Language of Uganda: An Arabic Creole in Africa*. Leiden: Brill.

Woidich, Manfred. 2006. *Das Kairenisch-Arabische: Eine Grammatik*. Wiesbaden: Harrassowitz.

Woodard, Roger D., ed. 2004. *The Cambridge Encyclopedia of the World's Ancient Languages*. Cambridge: Cambridge University Press.

Wright, W. [1896–98] 1967. *A Grammar of the Arabic Language, Translated from the German of Caspari*. 3d edn. Revised by W. Robertson Smith and M.J. de Goeje. 2 vols. Cambridge: Cambridge University Press.

Yarshater, Ehsan. 1998. The Persian Presence in the Islamic World. In *The Persian Presence in the Islamic World*, ed. Richard G. Hovannisian and Georges Sabagh, pp. 4–125. Cambridge: Cambridge University Press.

Zaborski, Andrzej. 2003. Arabic Loan-words. In *Encyclopaedia Aethiopica, Volume 1*, pp. 308–9. Wiesbaden: Harrassowitz.

Zemánek, Petr. 1996. *The Origins of Pharyngealization in Semitic*. Prague: Enigma.